John Cottingham was born in London and educated at Merchant Taylors' School and at St John's College, Oxford, where he gs in 'Mods' and 'Greats'; losophy at Oxford. He i *tion with Burman* (1976) an n of Descartes' *Philosophica* tributed many articles to ham has tought at the University of Washington, Seattle, and at Exeter College, Oxford; he is at present Lecturer in Philosophy at the University of Reading.

JOHN COTTINGHAM

RATIONALISM

GENERAL EDITOR
JUSTIN WINTLE

Granada Publishing

285559

Paladin Books
Granada Publishing Ltd
8 Grafton Street, London W1X 3LA

A Paladin Paperback Original 1984

Copyright © John Cottingham 1984

ISBN 0-586-08439-8

Reproduced, printed and bound in Great Britain by
Hazell Watson & Viney Limited, Aylesbury, Bucks

Set in Baskerville

16.1.87

CONTENTS

Contents

vii

'to D.C.B. and in
memoriam R.F.C.'

PREFACE

This book aims to provide a critical survey of philosophical rationalism from Plato to the present day, and is intended to be useful both to the general reader and to the student with a more specific interest in philosophy. A work of this type must steer a difficult course between on the one hand irking the specialist by oversimplification and on the other hand annoying the general reader by unnecessary technica- lities. In attempting to avoid both these hazards, I have tried to go into sufficient detail to do justice to the complex arguments involved, while at the same time avoiding minutiae of interpretation and keeping jargon to the mini- mum.

As will be evident from the detailed table of contents, the strategy followed is a selective rather than a comprehensive one. I have not tried to include all the thinkers who might reasonably be classed as 'rationalists', for the result would have been an endless recital of names and dates. Instead I have picked out the central figures – the most creative and exciting thinkers. Even within this narrowing of focus much has had to be omitted, for the ideas of the giants – precisely because they are giants – are vigorously resistant to com- pression.

A tiresome feature of many textbooks and reference works is that a thesis will often be attributed to a great thinker with little or no indication as to whether it is the original formulation, or a paraphrase, or a reconstruction or reinterpretation. In the present work, I have always tried to supply exact quotations and full references to original works wherever possible, so that the reader will be able to pin down the primary sources involved. Where an author or title is mentioned in a footnote followed by a number in square brackets (e.g. Aristotle, *Nicomachean Ethics* [20]), full details will be found in the Bibliography at the end of the book, under the appropriate number. The Bibliography also contains suggestions for further reading.

I am grateful to Oswald Wolff (Publishers) Ltd for permission to make use, in Chapter 3, of material from an essay on Leibniz which I originally wrote for their *German Men of Letters* series; and to Cambridge University Press for permission to make use, in Chapter 5, of material from my article 'Neonaturalism and its Pitfalls', which originally appeared in the journal *Philosophy*. I should also like to record my thanks to Professor Antony Flew, Professor G. H. R. Parkinson and Dr J. E. Tiles for many helpful comments and suggestions, and to Joan Morris for her speedy and efficient typing.

I

TERMS AND METHODS

It is often supposed that we should begin any enquiry by 'defining our terms'. But this ancient prejudice has little to commend it. If one wants to know what democracy is, understanding will not greatly be enhanced by dictionary definitions such as 'government of the people'. Much better to look in detail at how the assembly in ancient Athens worked, or at the detailed workings of the constitution and the electoral system in a modern liberal state. The same goes for 'rationalism'. The best way to understand this complex term is not to begin with tidy definitions but to look in detail at the specific arguments and theories of the major thinkers who make up the rationalist tradition. If one wants to understand and evaluate the rationalist world outlook, there is no substitute for working through the arguments of individual philosophers. Before we take the plunge, however, it will be necessary to clear away some initial ambiguities.

RATIONALISM AND ATHEISM

In the past, particularly in the seventeenth and eighteenth centuries, the term 'rationalist' was often used to refer to free thinkers of an anti-clerical and anti-religious outlook, and for a time the word acquired a distinctly pejorative force (thus in 1670 Sanderson spoke disparagingly of 'a mere rationalist, that is to say in plain English an Atheist of the late Edition . . .').[1] The use of the label 'rationalist' to characterize a world outlook which has no place for the supernatural is becoming less popular today; terms like 'humanist' and 'materialist' seem largely to have taken its place. But the old usage still survives: a recent essay on John Stuart Mill employs the term 'rationalist' and 'rationalism' to characterize Mill's secular freethinking outlook.[2]

The reader should be warned at the outset that the rationalism to be discussed in this book, 'rationalism' in the philosophical sense, must not be identified with rationalism in the secularist sense. In the first place, a rationalist in the sense of a secularist may well not be a rationalist in the technical philosophical sense. J. S. Mill is a case in point: though Mill was the 'patron saint of free-thinkers', his philosophical outlook is most certainly not 'rationalist' in the technical sense (in fact, it belongs firmly in the 'empiricist' tradition of Locke and Hume which, as will be explained later, is profoundly sceptical of the claims of philosophical rationalism). Conversely, and just as important, to be a rationalist in the philosophical sense need not in any way imply that one is committed to denying, or even sceptical about, the existence of God. On the contrary, as will emerge in the following chapters, some of the most famous rationalist philosophers placed God at the very centre of their systems of thought.

RATIONALISM AND REASON

If we leave aside questions about God, the most obvious and immediate association which the word 'rationalism' carries for the general reader is its association with the cognate adjective 'rational'. The etymological root from which both words are derived is the Latin noun *ratio*, meaning 'reason'. A 'rationalist' in the broadest sense is thus generally taken to be one who places special emphasis on man's rational capacities and has a special belief in the value and importance of reason and rational argument. Although this general notion of 'rationalism' is still a long way short of the technical sense of the term, it does bring us a little nearer to it, and so deserves a brief word of discussion.

2

A belief in the value and importance of rational argument is a prerequisite for all serious intellectual inquiry. Its earliest champion in the Western tradition was Socrates of Athens, who has a good claim to be regarded as the founding father of philosophy. Socrates constantly insisted that we must not be content with popular prejudice or accepted opinion, but must 'follow the argument where it leads'. Reason must be used both to analyse our beliefs and concepts and to subject them to critical scrutiny: 'the unexamined life is not worth living.'[3] This Socratic slogan was no idle boast: Socrates went to his death in 399 B.C. rather than give up his commitment to critical inquiry and the independent exercise of reason. Later in the fourth century, Aristotle put forward a theory of human nature which made rationality the defining characteristic of man. Man is a 'rational animal'. His capacities include not just nutritive faculties (which he shares with plants) and loco-motive and sensory faculties (which he shares with animals) but also a rational faculty: man not only feeds and moves and has sensations which make him aware of the environment, he also thinks and reasons. Our ability to reason – to organize our ideas in a coherent logical pattern – is the most distinctive and crucial of human capacities, and the one which distinguishes us from other sentient creatures. And in his *Ethics* Aristotle goes so far as to assert that man's supreme happiness consists in '*theoria*' – the exercise of purely theoretical powers of reasoning.[4]

The standards of rationality – logical precision, consistency, coherence, a commitment to 'follow the argument where it leads' – have not always met with universal approval. In the philosophy of Friedrich Nietzsche there is a progressive glorification of the 'Dionysian' element in human nature – the darker, more emotional side to our being which is contrasted with the purely rational 'Apollonian' element. Nietzsche speaks scathingly of the 'decadence' of Socrates, a decadence which, he says, 'is suggested by the hypertrophy of the logical faculty': 'The philosophers are the decadents of Greek culture . . . It is only in the

Dionysian mysteries, the psychology of the Dionysian state, that the basic fact of the Hellenic instinct finds its expression in its "will to life." '[5]

This scepticism about the value of pure rationality is enthusiastically endorsed by D. H. Lawrence: 'Real knowledge comes out of the whole corpus of the consciousness; out of your belly and your penis as much as out of your brain and mind. The mind can only analyse and rationalize. Set the mind and the reason to cock it over the rest, and all they can do is to criticize, and make a deadness.'[6]

Such attacks on rationality are anathema to many philosophers. Bertrand Russell, commenting on Lawrence's notion of a 'real', non-rational kind of knowledge (what Lawrence elsewhere called 'blood-knowing') observes drily: 'this seemed to me frankly rubbish, and I rejected it vehemently, though I did not know then that it led straight to Auschwitz'.[7] But while the Lawrentian attack on reason may be in part confused and dangerous, it is not wholly so. First, Russell's historical slur is unfair: Lawrence cannot be blamed for the activities of the Nazis (nor, incidentally, is it fair to construe Nietzsche's ideas as a justification for fascism, despite the fact that some Nazi propagandists attempted to interpret them in this way). Secondly, it may be said in defence of Lawrence that there are clearly many valuable and worile human activities whose appeal is not primarily rational or intellectual. Painting or dancing or eating are all good examples of worthwhile activities that do not require analytical, narrowly intellectual skills. The mind is, of course, involved in such activities, but their appeal is not to that part of us which is employed in, for example, logic or mathematics; indeed, the attempt to evaluate or analyse such activities by means of strictly logical categories may well blind us to much of their value. If this is what is meant by the Nietzschean and Lawrentian insistence on the limits of reason, then it is sensible and uncontroversial enough. The confusion comes in if we begin to take seriously Lawrence's claim that there is a 'real' non-rational kind of knowledge that comes from 'the blood'.

For knowledge, propositional knowledge or knowledge 'that . . .', necessarily relates to what is the case – to that which is true. And if we want, not merely to act and react in various interesting ways, not merely to paint and dance, but to make assertions that are supposed to be *true*, then the standards of rationality are inevitably required. To reject rationality is not, and cannot be, to pave the way for the development of a 'higher' or 'deeper' truth; instead it is simply to opt out of the whole business of making truth-claims. If any assertion is to have content, if it is to state something that is capable of being true, then it cannot avoid conforming to the canons of logic and rationality. At the very least, for example, an assertion 'P' must, in order to have content, rule out its opposite 'not P', for the very good reason that to assert both 'P' and 'not P' at the same time is to fail to make any assertion at all. The upshot is that the standards of rationality are not an optional luxury, or a narrow obsession of intellectuals; they are inescapably required by anyone whose aim is to *tell* us anything whatsoever. And this perforce applies to a Nietzsche as well as to a Socrates, to a D. H. Lawrence as well as to a Bertrand Russell.

TWO SENSES OF 'RATIONALISM'

The general and broad notion of 'rationalism' then, implies a commitment to the standards of rationality – a commitment which is an essential requirement for any philosophical system, and indeed for any set of truth-claims whatsoever. In this general sense it seems clear that all philosophers without exception are, or ought to be, rationalists. But this is very far from the case when we come to the more technical sense of 'rationalist', and hence great caution is needed when we shift from the general connotations of the term to its specific philosophical meaning. Thus, although Aristotle laid great stress on reason and rationality, this does not make him a 'rationalist' in the technical sense. Similarly, the thinkers of the European Enlightenment in the eighteenth century are often loosely described as 'rationalist', by which is meant that they were generally committed to the use of reason and argument in order to free philosophy from the chains of superstition and dogma; but this general use of the label can easily mislead, for only some of the Enlightenment philosophers are 'rationalists' in the technical sense. Leibniz, for instance, clearly belongs in the rationalist camp, while David Hume most certainly does not. The work of Bertrand Russell provides another example of the ambiguity in the label 'rationalist'. Russell's championing of reason and argument against the irrationalism of Lawrence makes it natural to call him a 'rationalist' in the broad sense; but most of his specific philosophical doctrines and methods belong firmly in the empiricist tradition and are thus almost entirely at odds with the rationalist outlook in the technical sense of that phrase.

RATIONALISM IN THE STRICT SENSE

Rationalism in its restricted and technical sense is invariably contrasted with empiricism, and although this distinction needs to be made with care if oversimplification is to be avoided, it remains a useful and indeed unavoidable starting point for any discussion of rationalist philosophy. Empiricism, from the Greek *empeiria* (experience) is a thesis about the nature and origins of human knowledge; there are many variations and distinct formulations, but essentially the claim is that all human knowledge derives ultimately from sensory experience. Rationalists, by contrast, stress the role played by reason as opposed to the senses in the acquisition of knowledge. Some rationalists condemn the senses as an inherently suspect and unreliable basis for knowledge claims; others, while conceding that sensory experience is in some sense necessary for the development of human knowledge, nevertheless insist that it can never be sufficient by itself. All rationalists characteristically maintain the possibility of *a priori* knowledge. This is sometimes defined as knowledge possessed *prior to* experience; but it is better to say that a proposition is known *a priori* if its truth can be established independently of any sensory observation. Empiricists tend to claim that the only propositions that we can know *a priori* are propositions of an ultimately uninformative kind – tautologies such as 'all bachelors are unmarried' which give no information about the world but depend solely on the definitions of the terms involved. The rationalist view is that *a priori* knowledge is by no means confined to tautologies. On the contrary, rationalists make the striking claim that by the light of reason we can, independently of experience, come to know certain important and substantive truths about reality, about the nature of the human mind and about the nature of the universe and what it contains.

THE PREJUDICE AGAINST RATIONALISM

The claims of rationalism to achieve substantive *a priori* knowledge will be examined in detail in the following chapters. But before we begin, it is as well to note an initial prejudice which many modern readers may have against the rationalist enterprise as so far outlined. It is probably fair to say that the average 'intelligent layman', particularly in the English-speaking world, has, whether consciously or subconsciously, absorbed a strongly empiricist outlook concerning human knowledge; and this is particularly true when it comes to natural science. The scientist's job, it is widely felt, is essentially an empirical one; scientific methods are, or ought to be, closely tied to actual observation and experimentation as opposed to abstract theorizing. Those who have this conception of the methodology of science may be inclined to dismiss the rationalist project of pure inquiry, independent of sensory experience, as a kind of self-indulgent and introverted game that can have little practical value. This attitude was forcefully articulated over three centuries ago by the arch-empiricist Francis Bacon who observed: 'empiricists are like ants; they collect and put to use; but rationalists, like spiders, spin threads out of themselves.'[8]

This rigid dichotomy between, on the one hand, sound empirical science which proceeds experimentally and, on the other, the fanciful *a priori* constructions of rationalism will not survive any serious examination of how science actually works. Recent developments in the history and philosophy of science make it increasingly difficult to maintain the simplistic equation between 'good science' and empirical observation. We shall have occasion to take a close look at some of these developments in Chapter 5, but for the present it will be enough to enter a warning that the empiricist account of science is very far from problem-free. At the risk of compressing matters grotesquely, just three of the difficulties which empiricism has to face may be mentioned. First, the path from 'observed facts' to 'scientific law' is beset with thorny logical problems to do with confirmation and strength of evidence; secondly, few of those whom we regard as 'good' scientists have in actual fact followed, or even attempted to follow, such a path; and, thirdly, the very notion of the 'empirical facts' and the 'observed data' is distinctly problematic.[9]

In the battle between rationalists and empiricists there is thus no reason at all to concede the victory to the empiricists in advance. Indeed one of the most fascinating features in the history of philosophy is the way in which philosophical disputes are resistant to being definitively 'settled'. The philosophical history of our own century provides a striking instance of this: the apparently unassailable dominance of the empiricist outlook in scientific and philosophical circles in the 1930s, '40s and '50s has now been sharply eroded, and some of the claims of rationalism have been reassessed in a more sympathetic light. These recent developments will be discussed in the final chapter. But the first task will be to trace the origins of rationalism in the classical period, and then go on and describe its development and flowering in the elaborate metaphysical systems of the seventeenth century.

RATIONALISM A 'CLUSTER CONCEPT'

The contrast drawn above between rationalism and empiricism may give the impression that philosophers can be neatly boxed into two exclusive compartments labelled respectively 'rationalists' and 'empiricists'. But this would be a dangerous oversimplification. In the first place, 'rationalism' does not denote one simple doctrine 'D', such that we can define rationalists as all and only those philosophers who subscribe to 'D'. Such exactness is seldom obtainable even in the case of more concrete concepts. We cannot say, for example, that all and only cats share some precise feature 'F' which makes them cats. Rather, there is a *cluster* of features: having four legs, fur, whiskers, a tail, being domesticated and so on. There may be paradigm cases of cats which possess all the standard features, but others may lack one or more of the features (wild cats, Manx cats), yet share a sufficient number of the other features to enable them to be classed as cats. In the history of rationalism we find a similar cluster of features. One strand in rationalism is *innatism*, which is itself a complex cluster of notions involving the idea that the mind is equipped from birth with certain fundamental concepts or with knowledge of certain fundamental truths. Another strand is *apriorism* – the belief in the possibility of arriving at knowledge independently of the senses. Another strand is *necessitarianism* – the notion that philosophy can uncover necessary truths about reality. And there are many other criss-crossing strands in what we call the 'rationalist' tradition. The emphasis will vary from philosopher to philosopher, and the features that make us inclined to classify a thinker as belonging to the rationalist tradition will not always be the same in every case.

A second caveat is that the labels 'rationalism' and 'empiricism' should not be regarded as marking out two precise areas of mutually exclusive territory. Often there will be a considerable degree of overlap, so that while a given philosopher matches the paradigm of rationalism in one respect, there may be other strands in his thought which are symptomatic of a more empiricist outlook. Some recent commentators have been so impressed with this phenomenon of overlap that they have suggested the labels 'rationalism' and 'empiricism' should be discarded, as being more trouble than they are worth. But this seems a misguided recommendation. There are many areas of overlap between the thought of Catholic and Protestant thinkers, but that is not a good reason for attempting to describe the history of religion without reference to these fundamental categories. And similarly, for better or worse, the label 'rationalism' is an indispensable tool for understanding the Western philosophical tradition. For, despite the problems of overlap and clustering, there is a recognizable tradition of rationalist philosophy, just as there is a recognizable tradition of Catholic theology, or, for that matter, a recognizable class of cats. We do not necessarily achieve philosophical insight by fastidiously avoiding labels which present problems of definition and precision. Labels can be useful and informative, provided we remember that what is involved is not a single, fixed 'essence' but, as Ludwig Wittgenstein put it, 'a complicated network of overlapping and criss-crossing similarities'.[10]

PHILOSOPHY AS DIALOGUE

Our aim in unravelling the various strands of rationalist thought from Plato to the present day will not be primarily a historical one; for any approach to philosophy that attempts to reduce it to mere 'history of ideas' – the laying out of ancient fossils for inspection – is unlikely to bear much fruit. This is not to say that chronology can be ignored: the tendency of some recent writers to lift philosophical ideas clean out of context and use them as target practice can lead to serious distortions. But the fact remains that in order to understand a philosopher, whether ancient or modern, we need to subject his ideas to continual critical scrutiny; we must, as it were, *argue with* the philosopher as opposed to imbibing his doctrines passively. To approach the subject in this way is to take seriously the Socratic insistence that the study of philosophy is essentially a *dialectical* business: it proceeds by dialogue, by argument and counter-argument, rather than by plain exposition. The suggestion that we can conduct a dialogue with the great rationalists of the past, with a Descartes or a Leibniz, may at first seem fanciful. But the enterprise starts to look much more feasible and interesting once one has begun to appreciate that many of the issues dealt with by these thinkers – the criteria for adequate knowledge, the nature of substance, the structure of the human mind – are still matters of intense philosophical debate today. One of the most distinctive characteristics – some would say *the* distinctive characteristic – of philosophical problems is their refusal to become obsolete, their power to fascinate and vex successive generations.

In scrutinizing the various elements of rationalist thought and evaluating the ideas involved, it is of course impossible to step outside the cultural and historical milieu in which we now find ourselves. And it would be rash and arrogant in the extreme to suppose that our own generation has produced the definitive solutions to some of the most central and long-standing problems of philosophy. But by comparing the approach of modern philosophers to that of their predecessors, and seeing how the problems have been reworked and reinterpreted, we may perhaps be able to deepen our understanding, and begin to distinguish what is important from what is peripheral, what are matters of enduring interest from what are temporary obsessions and aberrations. It may not be possible, or even desirable, to produce a set of ultimate answers; what matters is to continue the dialogue.

NOTES

N.B. Numbers in square brackets refer to items in the Bibliography.

1. Robert Sanderson, *Ussher's Power Princes* (1670) quoted in the *Oxford English Dictionary* s.v. 'rationalist'.

2. Bernard Crick, 'John Stuart Mill' in Wintle [97].
3. Plato, *Laws* [14] 667a; *Protagoras* [12] 333c; *Apology* [15] 38a5.
4. Aristotle, *Nichomachean Ethics* [24] Bk.I, Ch.7 and Bk.X.
5. Nietzsche [3], pp.475, 559, 561. For a more sympathetic view of what Nietzsche meant by his glorification of Dionysus see Kaufmann [4] Ch.4.
6. D.H. Lawrence, *Lady Chatterley's Lover* (1928), Ch.4.
7. *The Autobiography of Bertrand Russell* [5] Vol.II, p.22.
8. From *Cogitata et Visa* (1607) in [6] p.616. In fact Bacon goes on to talk of a middle way; that of the bee, who collects material but then transforms it.
9. See below, Ch.5, section F.
10. *Philosophical Investigations* [8] Part I, section 66.

THE CLASSICAL BACKGROUND

Rationalism is often described in textbooks as if it were a phenomenon that began and ended with the seventeenth century. This view is completely mistaken. In the first place, rationalist ideas and theories do, as we shall see, continue to exert considerable influence in many areas of philosophy today. And in the second place, the work of the great seventeenth-century rationalists did not spring out of nothing. In some respects, it is true, the work of Descartes or of Leibniz was strikingly new and original. But the philosophical shape of many of the problems that preoccupied them would have been unrecognizable without the classical Greek tradition which they inherited.

Of the two Greek philosophical giants, Aristotle is not usually classified as a rationalist, and, as will appear, his role in the development of rationalist thought is a complicated one. But it was the contribution of Plato that was decisive. Indeed, Plato's account of the nature and objects of true philosophical knowledge was so influential that he can in many respects be called the father of rationalism. So it is with Plato, and in particular with his theory of knowledge, that our inquiry must begin.

KNOWLEDGE AND BELIEF IN PLATO

The first step in any account of knowledge is to distinguish it from belief. It is obvious at an intuitive level that there is an important difference between knowing that something is the case and merely believing that it is so. One elementary point of difference is that knowledge is linked to truth: if someone qualifies as knowing a proposition then this implies that the proposition is true; beliefs, on the other hand, can be, and often are, false. But even when a belief is true, this does not necessarily qualify it as a piece of knowledge. I may believe that there is life on other worlds, and this belief may in fact happen to be true; but my belief does not therefore amount to knowledge. Knowledge, it seems, is an *improvement* on true belief; and one plausible account of this improvement is to say that the person who knows something does not merely have a true belief but can give some account which justifies or gives grounds for the belief, or explains *why* it is true.

This plausible and sensible first step in the analysis of knowledge was clearly articulated by Plato. In two of his dialogues, the *Theaetetus* and the *Meno*, we find the suggestion that knowledge improves on true belief in that the knower can give some sort of explanation of why his belief is true. In the *Theaetetus* Plato canvasses the view that knowledge is 'true belief with an *account*' (in Greek *logos*); while in the *Meno* we are told that knowledge involves being able to come up with explanatory *reasoning* (*logismos*).[1] (The Greek root *logos* which is involved in both these passages has a broad meaning and suggests on the one hand such notions as 'word', 'language' and 'definition', and on the other hand 'thought', 'reason' and 'rationality'.)

So far the Platonic account of knowledge is uncontroversial enough, although a great deal more detail would have to be supplied to make it precise. But there are other places where Plato wrestles with the distinction between knowledge and belief and comes up with an analysis the implications of which are much more remarkable. In the *Republic* (*circa* 380 B.C.) knowledge is said not just to consist in true belief supported by an explanation, but to be *infallible*.[2] Moreover knowledge and belief are classified as different 'powers' or 'faculties', from which Plato draws the (questionable) conclusion that they must have different objects. Plato goes on to explain this alleged difference in the objects of knowledge and belief by saying that know-ledge relates to what *is*, while belief relates to what 'is and is not'.[3]

Exactly what Plato is saying in this much-discussed passage is controversial. Some commentators have taken Plato to be making a claim about 'degrees of reality' or 'grades of existence': in this view he is suggesting that the objects of knowledge exist in some special, privileged sense, while the objects of belief hover about uneasily in a twilight world half way between existence and non-existence. It is difficult to know what to make of this curious notion; but fortunately a simpler and more plausible interpretation is suggested by what Plato has to say later on about the objects of belief. When we have a belief about a beautiful individual, or a just action, there is, Plato suggests, a difficulty which arises from the fact that what is supposed to be beautiful or just may, from another point of view, be ugly or unjust. Helen of Troy may be beautiful this year, but in thirty years' time she may be ugly; an action like returning borrowed property may be just in some cases, but in other cases (returning a weapon to a dangerous madman) it may be unjust. Similarly, says Plato, 'things which are large or heavy may equally well, from another point of view, be called small or light'.[4] Our conventional beliefs about the world thus suffer, according to Plato, from a crucial defect: when we ascribe some property 'F' to some object in the world it may well turn out that, though the object is 'F' from one point of view, it is 'not-F' from some other standpoint. This argument, the 'argument from opposites' as it is sometimes called, thus purports to show that the properties ascribed to the objects of belief are always subject to revision and qualification: such objects never possess their properties in an absolute and unqualified way.

If the ordinary objects of belief can only be said to be just or beautiful, or large or heavy, in a qualified or restricted way, then the next question is whether there is anything which can count as unqualifiedly beautiful or just, or large or heavy. Plato's answer is a firm 'yes'. His argument has paved the way for the introduction of the so-called 'Forms', the 'eternal, unchanging, absolute realities',[5] which he claims to be the true objects of knowledge.

THE FORMS: UNCHANGING REALITY AND PURE UNDERSTANDING

Plato's references to the Forms, which are scattered through the *Republic* and various other dialogues, do not always appear consistent. Sometimes he implies that whenever we apply a term 'F' to a group or class of objects there must be a *Form of 'F'* from which the objects in question derive their F-ness. Thus, in addition to the various particular beds made by various carpenters there is an absolute Form of Bed, which was made by God; and it is participation in this Form which gives a particular item its essential character as a bed. In other places (e.g. in the *Parmenides*) Plato expresses some doubts about whether there is a corresponding Form corresponding to all general terms (is there a Form of 'mud' or of 'filth', for example?). The commonly used label 'the *theory* of Forms' suggests that Plato deploys a fully worked out set of doctrines, and it may well be (as recent Plato scholarship suggests) that his views are less systematic and less fully worked out than such talk of 'the *theory* of Forms' tends to imply.[6] But there is one central strand that is crucial for our purposes, and that is the following: in addition to the objects of belief, the particular items that are the subject-matter of our ordinary judgements about the world around us, Plato holds that there are also objects of knowledge which possess their properties in an absolute and unqualified way. Over and above the various particular things that are, e.g. beautiful, there is what Plato calls 'the beautiful itself', that which is beautiful in an eternal, unchanging and unqualified way. And it is this – the Form of the beautiful as opposed to particular beautiful things – that is the object of philosophical knowledge.

Now it is at once apparent that an object such as 'the beautiful itself' – absolute unqualified beauty – is not something that is encountered in ordinary everyday life. It cannot be observed by the senses; rather it is something whose nature is wholly abstract or theoretical, and which must therefore be grasped not visibly or tangibly but purely intellectually. And this brings us to the decisive step in Plato's reasoning that makes it appropriate to call him the father of rationalism: true knowledge, Plato insists, requires a move away from the sensible world to the world of 'intelligibles'. What is involved here is a fundamental contrast between the sensible world – the ordinary world revealed to us by the five senses – and a separate world of *intelligibilia* – a world whose objects must be apprehended by the intellect alone. This notion is developed by Plato in terms of his famous similes of the sun, the divided line and the cave. These similes have given rise to a vast literature of interpretation and criticism; but the briefest of summaries should here be enough to bring out the main contrast which Plato is urging upon us. The simile of the sun contrasts the visible world with the intelligible world (the world of the Forms): just as the sun gives visibility to the objects of the senses, so the supreme Form (which Plato identifies with the Form of the Good) gives intelligibility to the objects of knowledge. The contrast is expanded and sharpened in the simile of the 'divided line', the central point of which is that the relationship between a physical object and its shadow is analogous to the relationship between the objects of the intellect (the Forms) and the objects of ordinary belief. Thus the person who is preoccupied with particular judgements about the physical world is in a sense dealing with mere shadows. To achieve knowledge he must move away from the ordinary sense-perception and direct his mind upwards to the objects of pure understanding. Finally, in the graphic simile of the cave, Plato likens the life of the ordinary man to that of chained prisoners watching flickering images projected against the wall of an underground cavern. First of all, says Plato, the prisoners 'must be freed from the bonds and cured of their delusions' (presumably this involves freeing the mind from blind prejudice and constructing a set of true beliefs about the world). But this is only the beginning of wisdom. To make the move from mere belief to true knowledge, the would-be philosopher must be dragged out of the cave altogether; he must move up and away from the murkiness of the physical world to the higher world of light and sunshine which represents the realm of knowledge and the Forms. Once out of the cave he can embark on the path to knowledge, and ultimately he will be able to contemplate the Forms in all their truth and beauty: 'the ascent into the upper world and to the sight of the objects there may be compared to the upward progress of the mind to the intelligible world.'[7]

Part of the purpose behind these similes is a political one. Plato's aim in the *Republic* is to show that the just state must necessarily be governed by those who possess true knowledge – the philosophers: 'the society we have described will never be a reality . . . and we will see no end to the troubles of humanity until philosophers become the kings . . .'[8] Many of Plato's critics, both ancient and modern, have been highly sceptical about the practicability and indeed the desirability of entrusting government to a philosophical élite. But if the political aspects of Plato's theory are left aside, there remains an extraordinarily evocative picture of the road to true knowledge which has had a profound influence on philosophy in general, and the rationalist tradition in particular. What Plato's claim boils down to is that the achievement of true knowledge requires a systematic attempt to free the mind from the everyday world of the senses, from the world of empirical observation and common-sense belief.

PLATO'S APRIORISM

Plato's rejection of the senses as a source of knowledge comes out with particular clarity when he describes his programme of education for prospective philosopher-rulers. The whole purpose of the Platonic curriculum is to 'draw the mind away from the senses' towards the pure exercise of *a priori* reasoning: 'Arithmetic is useful for our purposes. For it draws the mind upwards and forces it to argue about pure numbers, and will not be put off by any attempt to confine the argument to collections of visible or tangible objects.'[9] After arithmetic comes geometry, and then, surprisingly, astronomy. But it turns out to be 'astronomy' of an extremely abstract and unempirical kind: 'We shall treat astronomy like geometry and *ignore the visible heavens* if we want to direct the mind to a useful purpose.'[10] In Plato's conception, the actual behaviour of celestial bodies is thus irrelevant. True knowledge comes not from observation of the visible world but from abstract mathematical reasoning. (This conception should not be dismissed as wholly bizarre: modern astronomers, it should be noted, seek for and employ highly abstract mathematical laws which are not observed by the senses – though they are of course correlated with sensory phenomena by a long process of reasoning.)

Plato's system of knowledge is not wholly mathematical. Some of the Forms, like the Form of Justice and the Form of Beauty, are certainly not mathematical objects. And elsewhere Plato suggests that mathematical reasoning is a means to an end rather than an end in itself. But mathematical studies are constantly invoked as a crucial step towards the kind of abstract reasoning to which a philosopher must accustom himself before he can achieve knowledge. Plato suggests that philosophical knowledge is concerned not with what happens to be the case but with what cannot be otherwise; as he puts it, it is concerned with 'eternal reality, the reality unaffected by change and decay'.[11] Moreover, such knowledge is not *a posteriori*, not derived from experience, but *a priori*, derived from abstract reasoning independently of the senses. As Plato puts it 'one must strive to reach ultimate realities by the exercise of pure reason without any aid from the senses'.[12] The resulting picture is a striking and in some ways a seductive one. It holds out the hope that philosophy can achieve insight into eternal, absolute truths that transcend the world of contingency and happenstance. And it is a conception that, as we shall see, gave a powerful impetus to the development of the philosophical systems of the great European rationalists.

PROBLEMS WITH THE PLATONIC CONCEPTION OF KNOWLEDGE

(i) Infallibility and necessity. We have noted that Plato regards knowledge as (a) infallible and (b) concerned with 'eternal reality'. The acceptance of these claims by later philosophers led to the development of one of the standard tenets of rationalism: that knowledge cannot be concerned with contingent truths (propositions which *happen* to be true), but must deal exclusively with necessary truths (propositions which *must* be true). Whether this distinction should be read back into Plato is not clear; he certainly does not discuss it explicitly (and an alternative interpretation of Plato's account of knowledge will be mentioned below). But it will be useful to say a word here about the difficulties which beset the restriction of knowledge to the realm of necessary truths.

Many philosophers who have insisted that knowledge must be concerned with necessary truths seem to have been guilty of a logical blunder. It is one thing to claim that there is a necessary connection between knowledge and truth, but quite another to claim that knowledge must relate to necessary truth. To suppose that the first claim entails the second claim is fallacious, and the fallacy (which may be termed the 'modal shift' fallacy) can be explained as follows. It is a necessary truth that if Smith knows that P (where 'P' stands for any proposition you like), then P is true. To make a knowledge claim is automatically to commit oneself to the truth of what is asserted. This is quite straightforward: it is simply a function of the way in which the verb 'to know' operates. We may express this as:

(1) 'Necessarily [if S knows that P, then P is true].' But it is fallacious to shift the modal operator 'necessarily' forwards and to infer that:

(2) 'If S knows that P, then P is necessarily-true.' The

mistake here can perhaps be elucidated by an analogy. If a course of medical treatment is to count as a *cure*, then it is a necessary requirement that it be successful. This is quite straightforward: it is simply a function of the way in which the word 'cure' operates. We may express this as:

(1a) 'Necessarily [if X is a cure, then X is successful].'
But it is fallacious to shift the modal operator 'necessarily' forwards and infer that:

(2a) 'If X is a cure, then X is a necessarily-successful treatment.' Statement (2a) implies that a treatment can only count as a cure if its success can be logically guaranteed, and this suggests something highly dubious: that we should restrict the label 'cure' to treatments which are infallible, which cannot-but-succeed. But this is an impossibly stringent requirement. All that the original proposition (1a) says is that a cure is a treatment which *does in actual fact* succeed. And this is not at all to imply that a treatment can only count as a cure if it carries some infallible logical guarantee of success.

It should be noted that Plato himself does not commit the type of fallacy just described. But by his talk of knowledge as 'infallible' and as having 'eternal reality' as its object, he did, whether intentionally or not, pave the way for the restriction of the objects of knowledge to objects which possess their properties in a strictly necessary way. And, as the above discussion shows, such a restriction involves a *redefinition* of the verb 'to know'. We are being asked to accept a revised concept of knowledge such that only necessarily true propositions such as 'two plus two make four' or the 'Form of Justice is absolutely just' can count as knowable. But the ordinary concept of knowledge allows that propositions can be known if they are *in fact* true, even though their truth is not a matter of necessity. Empirical observations such as 'the sun is shining' or 'the cat sat on the mat' are not necessary truths: they are contingent assertions which may or may not be true, depending on the circumstances. But the Platonist has given no convincing argument for excluding such contingent, empirical propositions from the sphere of knowledge. And common sense suggests that we often have perfectly adequate grounds for asserting that such propositions are true, and that we are thus quite justified in claiming to know them.

An alternative interpretation. Some commentators have defended Plato against this type of criticism by suggesting that he wishes not so much to exclude empirical propositions from his conception of knowledge as to suggest that we must *go beyond* them, or *transcend* them if we are to achieve true understanding. On this view, Plato is concerned to show that true philosophical wisdom must involve not simply knowing what is true, but *understanding why* it is true (there are many places where the Greek verb *epistasthai* employed by Plato seems closer to our concept of 'understanding' rather than simply 'knowing'). In the *Republic*, Plato describes a special method for coming to understand reality which he calls 'dialectic'. Dialectic involves an 'upward ascent' of the mind to first principles; but once it has reached up to grasp the first principle, the mind, says Plato, 'may turn back and, holding on to the consequences which depend on it, descend at last to a conclusion'.[13] This is a difficult passage to interpret, but at least part of what Plato is saying seems to be that understanding must be *systematic*: a proposition must be fitted into some general theoretical structure if we are to come to appreciate why it is true. On this account Plato can be acquitted of the charge of arbitrarily restricting and redefining the concept of knowledge. Instead, he can be seen as offering a dynamic, dialectical concept of human understanding, which contains glimmerings of what has come to be known as a 'holistic' account of explanation – the kind of account later developed in the work of such rationalists as Spinoza.[14] Reality cannot be apprehended piecemeal: the philosopher must have a unified grasp of how each part fits into the whole if he is to be able to understand why things are the way they are, and thus achieve true understanding. As we shall see in the next two chapters, many of the debates between rationalists and empiricists in the seventeenth and eighteenth centuries centre around the question of whether such a unified understanding of reality is possible.

(ii) The status of mathematics. Another problem with Plato's approach to knowledge arises in connection with his enthusiasm for mathematical reasoning. Mathematical propositions are indeed timelessly and necessarily true, but this does not of itself entail that they have the status of categorical or 'absolute' truths. The necessity of the theorems of Euclidian geometry, for example, simply depends on the fact that they are deduced by logically watertight reasoning from Euclid's axioms. But what of the axioms themselves? The axioms are the initial *postulates* (or basic premises) of the system: they cannot themselves be demonstrated on pain of an infinite regress (they would have to be shown to follow from prior axioms and so on *ad infinitum*).[15] The upshot is that the status of mathematical truths appears to be *hypothetical* rather than categorical. They are, necessarily, true *if* the axioms are true; but they are not true in any 'absolute' sense. (Euclid's theorems, in fact, are quite properly expressed in a hypothetical form: '*if* such and such a figure is constructed then such and such properties will obtain . . .') So it may be possible to demonstrate quite different theorems on the basis of different initial definitions and postulates. This point is particularly clear to us nowadays in the light of the development of alternative, non-Euclidean geometrical systems, which are just as valid as Euclid's system, but which are constructed from different sets of initial axioms.

Interestingly, Plato himself concedes the hypothetical character of mathematical reasoning: 'students of geometry and similar forms of reasoning begin by taking certain things for granted . . . and treat them as basic assumptions.'[16] But so far from revising his own claims about the possibility of absolute non-hypothetical knowledge, Plato instead concludes that the kind of knowledge offered by mathematicians is limited by its hypothetical status: 'Although subjects like geometry are concerned with reality they only see it in a kind of dream and never clearly, so long as they leave their assumptions unquestioned'.[17] The philosopher, Plato insists, must transcend the conditional and hypothetical procedures of the mathematician. He must practise a special kind of rational activity which Plato calls *noesis* or 'pure thought': 'Pure thought treats its assumptions not as given but as . . . starting points and steps in the ascent to the universal self-sufficient first principle.'[18]

This upward ascent of pure thought to ultimate and absolute truth – to what Plato calls the self-sufficient or 'unhypothetical' first principle – is central to the rationalist outlook. And it involves a striking claim: that *a priori* reasoning can provide us not just with conceptual truths which follow from given definitions and postulates, but with substantive truths about reality. This is one of the most controversial claims in the history of philosophy, and consideration of it will be deferred until we look at how it is developed in the systems of the later rationalists. The point to notice here is that the ambitious programme of using *a priori* reasoning to discover the structure of absolute reality was Plato's brainchild. It was Plato who thought up the grand design – the upward ascent of pure thought until, as he puts it, it is finally able to 'set about the definition of the essential nature of reality'.[19]

PLATO AND THE DOCTRINE OF INNATE KNOWLEDGE

Before we leave Plato, one further element in his approach to knowledge must be noted. If philosophical knowledge arises 'without the aid of the senses', then it is natural to ask where, in that case, it does come from. If not observation of the world around us, then what *is* the source of our knowledge of ultimate reality? To say that the student of philosophy must be taught such truths by his teacher or mentor is scarcely an answer, since it merely shifts the question back to the previous generation. And in any case, Plato's dynamic or 'dialectical' conception of philosophical inquiry totally rejects the idea that knowledge can be passed on to a passive recipient in this way: 'we must reject the conception of education professed by those who say that they can put into the mind knowledge that was not there before.' Instead, says Plato, 'our argument indicates that this capacity [for grasping ultimate truths] is innate in each man's mind'.[20]

In the *Meno* and elsewhere, this doctrine of innate mental powers is explained in terms of the myth of *anamnesis* or 'recollection'. The soul is immortal and has seen all things in its previous voyaging. So what we call 'learning' is merely a recollection or reminiscence – a recovery of that lapsed knowledge which the soul remembers from its previous incarnations.[21] This strange doctrine is probably one of the best known of Plato's ideas, and its influence can be clearly seen in, amongst other places, Wordsworth's famous Ode:

> Our birth is but a sleep and a forgetting:
> The Soul that rises with us, our life's Star
> Hath had elsewhere its setting,
> And cometh from afar:
> Not in entire forgetfulness,
> And not in utter nakedness,
> But trailing clouds of glory do we come . . .[22]

But evocative though it may be for the poets, the explanatory value of the doctrine of *anamnesis* from a philosophical point of view is thin. To push back the acquisition of knowledge to a previous existence merely shelves the problem of how we come to know *a priori* truths rather than solving it.

However, Plato's doctrine of innate knowledge does have some plausible arguments to back it up. One important point is that it is difficult to see how our grasp of, for example, mathematical truths can be explained on the basis of sensory observation. In the *Phaedo*, for example, Plato points out that we have a concept of perfect mathematical equality, even though no two things we observe in our ordinary experience are ever perfectly equal.[23] And in the *Meno* Plato attempts to demonstrate that a young slave boy can be induced to see a truth of geometry (the example concerns the properties of a square) on the basis of his innate grasp of certain basic mathematical ideas. According to Plato, the slave, though untaught, had all the right insights already inside him; the teacher, like a midwife, merely had to 'draw the knowledge out' by asking the right questions.[24]

The empiricist critic may be highly sceptical here, and may suspect that in 'drawing out' the knowledge the teacher must in fact have employed leading questions in order to get the answer he wanted. And, in general, the empiricist will insist that mathematical concepts are acquired in infancy by means of the appropriate sensory stimuli. To which the rationalist will reply that no matter how skilfully he manipulates the bricks and the counters, a teacher will be unable to get a child to learn the simplest of mathematical truths unless the child already possesses an innate grasp of the underlying principles and connections involved. We shall return to these issues later, rather than trying to settle them here.[25] But this preliminary skirmish should be enough to indicate what an important role Plato's doctrine of innateness plays in the rationalist account of knowledge.

ARISTOTLE'S CRITIQUE OF PLATO

If the role of Plato as the founder of rationalism is clearly demonstrable, the contribution of Aristotle is much more ambiguous. It is often claimed that Aristotle is the founder of empiricism, which gives us the splendidly neat picture of one of the two Greek philosophical giants standing at the head of each of the great rival armies of rationalists and empiricists. But matters are seldom as simple as this in philosophy.

It is undoubtedly true that Aristotle had a distinctly unplatonic interest in the detailed behaviour and structure of the ordinary objects in the observable world. The vast corpus of Aristotelian scientific works, particularly in the area of natural history, contains a wealth of data based on empirical observation. And if one looks in general at Aristotle's approach to ontology – the question of what there is in the world – then it is immediately clear that his position is very much more down to earth than Plato's. For Aristotle, a substance (the ultimate bearer of qualities) is not an abstract Form but a concrete individual – for example a particular man or horse. In the *Metaphysics* Aristotle explicitly denies that a universal (e.g., beauty) can be a substance; and elsewhere he pours scorn on the notion that there can be such things as the 'Form of the Good', or 'absolute goodness'.[26] Goodness, for Aristotle, is not something transcendent; it is something which must be embodied or instantiated in particular good things. This approach suggests that an obvious starting point for many areas of philosophical inquiry is to look at the everyday objects in the world around us. And we often see Aristotle (for example in his treatises on ethics) suggesting that an investigation of a given topic should begin with a survey of the 'received opinions' – the standard views and commonsense beliefs which are held on a particular topic.[27]

All this seems at first sight to be far removed from Plato's abstract intellectualism and disdain for the senses. But a general interest in empirical observation is not of itself sufficient to justify labelling Aristotle as an empiricist. We need to ask much more precise and specific questions. Did Aristotle regard the senses as the ultimate basis of all human knowledge? And what was his attitude to the possibility of *a priori* knowledge?

On the first question, Aristotle is often credited with having formulated the empiricist doctrine that 'there is nothing in the intellect that was not previously in the senses'. This slogan, generally known in its Latin form, *nihil in intellectu quod non prius fuerit in sensu*, denies the possibility of an innate knowledge and insists that all our concepts are ultimately derived from sense-experience. The Latin maxim is to be found in the writings of Thomas Aquinas, and Aquinas certainly believed that in defending the empiricist doctrine he was following the authority of Aristotle, but a search through the Aristotelian corpus reveals no exact Greek equivalent to the Latin phrase used by Aquinas. However, Aristotle does suggest, in the *De Anima*, that the ability to understand requires the ability to form mental images; and this in turn requires the faculty of sense perception ('unless one perceived things one would not learn or understand anything').[28] So Aristotle's account of the workings of the mind is empiricist in so far as he believes that all knowledge ultimately presupposes an ability to perceive the world around us by means of the senses.

ARISTOTLE'S ACCOUNT OF DEMONSTRATIVE KNOWLEDGE

On the question of *a priori* knowledge, however, it is by no means clear that Aristotle rejects the Platonic view that reason can provide us with substantive necessary truths about the world. If we look at Aristotle's general account of scientific reasoning (in the *Posterior Analytics*) it turns out to be strongly influenced by an axiomatic or deductive conception of knowledge. Instead of insisting on inductive procedures based on sensory observations, like such later empiricists as Francis Bacon, Aristotle argues that true scientific knowledge must involve strict logical demonstrations from first principles: 'Since it is impossible for that of which there is [scientific] knowledge to be otherwise, what is known in virtue of demonstrative knowledge must be necessary. A demonstration therefore is a deduction [*syllogismos*] from necessary premises.'[29]

This looks like a firm commitment to the Platonic thesis that knowledge of reality is knowledge of necessary truths. Some commentators have tried to resist this apparently rationalistic bias in Aristotle's account of scientific reasoning by suggesting that all Aristotle really means to say is that the conclusions of a scientific argument follow necessarily from their premises (as is the case with any valid argument); and this need not imply that the premises are *themselves* necessary. Now it is certainly true that a deductive account of scientific reasoning (one that insists that conclusions be logically deduced from premises) *need* not imply a commitment to the controversial view that the premises themselves are necessary. But Aristotle himself undoubtedly does have such a commitment. He asserts quite explicitly that science is concerned with 'what cannot be otherwise'; in other words, he maintains a strongly necessitarian view of scientific truth. For Aristotle, the ultimate principles of science are not, as in the standard empiricist view, 'brute facts' – mere contingent assertions that might have been otherwise. On the contrary, science is concerned not with what happens to be true but with what *must* be true: 'scientific knowledge comes from necessary starting points, for what is known cannot be otherwise.'[30]

Aristotle readily admits that these ultimate starting points cannot themselves be demonstrated by logical deduction (if they were, they would not be the ultimate principles of the system: all demonstration must stop somewhere). How then are they to be known? Aristotle states in the *Posterior Analytics* that the first principles of science are known by a process called *epagoge*; and *epagoge* is often mentioned, alongside deductive reasoning (*syllogismos*) as one of the two ways in which we learn.[31] Now *epagoge* is normally translated as 'induction', but we should beware of being misled here and foisting on Aristotle the Baconian view that science establishes its results by 'inducing' general laws from careful observations and experiments in particular cases. In fact there is nothing in Aristotle that corresponds to a systematic 'experimental method' in science. The Greek word *epagoge* comes from the verb *epagogein* which has the ordinary, non-technical meaning of 'to lead on'; thus the fundamental idea in Aristotelian *epagoge* is that of the mind being 'lead on' from one truth to another.[32] It seems then that the role of the senses in establishing first principles is for Aristotle only a heuristic one. The senses may guide us in the right direction, or stimulate us to think along fruitful lines. But they cannot in themselves establish the truth of necessary propositions – they cannot provide us with knowledge of 'what cannot be otherwise' (*epagoge*, Aristotle insists, cannot by itself lead us to true knowledge or *episteme*). How then can we achieve knowledge of these ultimate necessities? Aristotle's solution is that we know scientific principles by rational intuition, the faculty which he calls *nous* – a word closely connected with Plato's term for pure rational apprehension *noesis*.[33] So despite the conventional picture of Aristotle as the defender of empiricism against Platonic rationalism, the model of scientific knowledge which he eventually comes up with seems heavily indebted to the *a priori*, necessitarian model of Plato.

RECENT REINTERPRETATIONS OF ARISTOTLE

It is worth noting that recent scholarship has suggested that it may be possible to interpret Aristotle's theory of deductive scientific knowledge in a rather different light. In the view of one modern critic, Aristotle is not really concerned to give an account of the logic of scientific discovery; his purpose in the *Posterior Analytics* is not to explain how scientists should proceed in their search for truth, but to describe the correct method for *teaching* or *imparting* knowledge: '. . . the theory of demonstrative science was never meant to guide or formalize research; it is concerned exclusively with the teachings of facts already won; it does not describe how scientists do, or ought to, acquire knowledge: it offers a formal model of how teachers should *present* and *impart* knowledge.'[34]

In yet another recent view, the Aristotelian model is designed to formulate the conditions for scientific *explanation*. To explain a phenomenon is to understand why it occurs, and this in turn involves showing that it is deducible from self-explanatory first principles: 'When Aristotle says that *episteme* [usually translated 'knowledge'] is concerned with what cannot be otherwise, his claim should be read not . . . as an unexamined legacy of Plato but as a substantive thesis designed to elucidate a current concept of understanding. That understanding is constituted by knowing the explanation of necessary connections in nature.'[35]

It is beyond the scope of this volume to examine these reconstructions of Aristotle's philosophy of science. But however we interpret Aristotle, it cannot be denied that he is committed to the claim that science does at some point involve the apprehension of necessary truths about reality or necessary connections in the natural world. It is this element in Aristotle's thinking that makes it appropriate to classify his approach as in some sense a 'rationalistic' one (and as we shall see, the idea of necessary truth and necessary connections is one which bulks large in the thought of the great seventeenth-century rationalists).

Since this necessitarian approach to science may strike many readers as bizarre and obviously misguided, it is perhaps worth pointing out that philosophers today are by no means agreed that it is wholly untenable. In the 1930s and '40s, when a radically empiricist philosophy of science was dominant, most philosophers would have insisted that science can only be concerned with contingent facts, and would have condemned utterly the Aristotelian notion that scientific knowledge relates to what 'cannot be otherwise'. Recent philosophical developments however have made the Aristotelian model look less implausible. For one thing, considerable doubt has been cast on whether a hard and fast line can be drawn between 'analytic' (necessarily true and unrevisable) propositions and 'synthetic' judgements (those concerned with the contingent facts of experience). Secondly, the whole notion of 'necessity' in science has undergone fresh scrutiny, and some philosophers now believe that it is possible for scientists to uncover 'real' necessities; that is, it is claimed that science may go beyond mere contingent correlations and investigate the *essential* properties of things – properties which 'cannot be otherwise'. We shall look at these developments in the final chapter.[36]

RATIONALISM AND ETHICS IN PLATO AND ARISTOTLE

It may be useful to conclude this survey of the classical antecedents of rationalism with a brief word on rationalism as it applies to the practical questions of ethics (as opposed to theoretical questions of philosophical or scientific truth). Plato's view of ethical notions such as justice and goodness is that we apprehend them *a priori* as ultimate Forms; hence, for Plato, there is no essential difference between the way in which we study goodness and the way in which we study the abstract truths of logic or mathematics; truth and goodness are ultimately linked together as aspects of the Supreme Form which is the source of all reality.

A traditional empiricist criticism of the rationalist theory of ultimate truth is that reason can only tell us what follows from what – it cannot tell us what is 'absolutely' true. And the corresponding empiricist criticism in the practical sphere is that reason can only tell us about *means*, not about ends: it can tell us what to do *if* we desire such and such an end, but it cannot of itself tell us what ends we ought to desire. 'Reason alone', as Hume succinctly puts it, 'can never produce any action or give rise to volition . . . Reason is and ought only to be the slave of the passions.'[37] This empiricist criticism of reason and its limitations in the practical sphere is neatly summed up in the ancient Latin tag '*intellectus nihil movet*' which may be freely translated, 'the intellect does not of itself initiate anything'. Reason can tell you how to get to your destination, but not what your destination should be.

The slogan '*intellectus nihil movet*' is in fact a direct translation from Aristotle. But those who cite this phrase as an indication of Aristotle's 'empiricist' approach to ethics fail to observe that it is only part of a sentence. If the relevant passage is quoted in full it reads, 'the intellect does not initiate anything of itself except when it is the practical intellect, which aims at an end'.[38] What Aristotle goes on to suggest is that, as well as working out means to desired ends, the intellect or reason does have a role in determining the ends themselves. He would not accept Hume's view that reason is merely the pimp or janitor of the passions. The crucial point, ignored by those who lump Aristotle with Hume, is that the virtuous man, in Aristotle's scheme, does not take his ends or goals for granted: he has to test his conduct to see if it is in accordance with the right rule (the *orthos logos*). And the determination of the right rule is, it seems, to be made in the light of an overall, rationally ordered, conception of the good life. It is the job of what Aristotle calls the *phronimos* – the man of practical wisdom – to use his rational powers to work out such an overall conception of the good life.[39]

To give a detailed account of Aristotle's subtle and complex conception of ethical reasoning would take us too far from the present purpose. But it should be clear even from this summary that to characterize Aristotle as 'anti-rationalist' is as misleading in the ethical sphere as it is in the sphere of scientific knowledge. This is not of course to say that Aristotle is a mere disciple of Plato. In many respects he draws back from the full-blooded rationalism of his teacher. To cite but two examples: Aristotle, as already noted, firmly rejects the theory of transcendental absolutes or Forms; and secondly, he resists the Platonic view that all knowledge is interconnected (insisting, for example, that ethics and science have different methods and aim at different levels of precision).[40] Nevertheless it is instructive to see how Aristotle, original and creative genius though he undoubtedly was, is often drawn back in spite of himself to the seductive Platonic vision of philosophy as a hierarchical system whose first principles are established by the light of reason. We shall see in the following chapters just how enduring that vision proved to be.

NOTES

1. *Theaetetus* 200/1 (see Cornford [10]); *Meno* 97/8 (see Sesonske [13]).
2. *Republic* 477e (see Lee [11]). Cf. *Theaetetus* 152c.

3. *Republic* 479.
4. *Ibid.*
5. *Ibid.*
6. See Annas, *An Introduction to Plato's Republic* [16] Ch.8.
7. *Republic* 517.
8. *Ibid.* 473.
9. *Ibid.* 525.
10. *Ibid.* 530.
11. *Ibid.* 485.
12. *Ibid.* 532.
13. *Ibid.* 511.
14. See below, Ch.3. For this more favourable interpretation of Plato's view cf. Annas [16] Chs.8, 9.
15. It should be noted that Euclid's canonization of geometry did not occur until several generations after Plato; the notion that geometry rests on *postulates* does not occur in Plato or Aristotle.
16. *Republic* 510.
17. *Ibid.* 533.
18. *Ibid.* 511.
19. *Ibid.* 511.
20. *Ibid.* 518.
21. *Meno* 18.
22. William Wordsworth, 'Ode, Intimations of Immortality from Recollections of Early Childhood' (1807).
23. *Phaedo* 72/7 (see Tredennick [15]).
24. *Meno* 82bff.
25. See below, Ch. 4, section A and Ch.5, section D.
26. *Metaphysics* Z 13 (1036b6) (see Smith and Ross [22]); *Nicomachean Ethics* Bk. I, Ch.6 (see Thompson [24]).
27. *Nicomachean Ethics* Bk. I, Ch.7.
28. *De Anima* III 8 (see Hamlyn [23a]).
29. *Posterior Analytics* I, 4 (73a21) (see Barnes [23b]).
30. *Ibid*, 6 (74b5).
31. *Ibid*, 12 (78a34) and I, 18 (81a40). Cf. *Nicomachean Ethics* Bk. VI, 3 (1139b26/8).
32. For more on Aristotle's notion of *epagoge* see Ross [27] 38ff; and Barnes, 'Aristotle's Theory of Demonstration', in *Articles on Aristotle* [28] Vol.I, pp.77ff.
33. *Post. An.* II, 19 (100b5); cf. Plato *Republic* 511. For more on Aristotle's philosophy of science see Ackrill [25] Ch.7.
34. Barnes [28] p.77.
35. M.F. Burnyeat, 'Aristotle on Understanding Knowledge', in *Aristotle on Science: The Posterior Analytics* [29].
36. See below, Ch.5, section C.

37. Hume, *A Treatise of Human Nature* (1739–40) [72] Bk. II, Part 3, section iii.
38. *Nicomachean Ethics* Bk. VI (1139a36). See also Bambrough, *Moral Scepticism and Moral Knowledge* [134] Ch.9.
39. *Nicomachean Ethics* Bk. VI and Bk. II, Ch.6. See also Richard Sorabji, 'Aristotle on the Role of Intellect in Virtue' in Rorty [30].
40. *Nichomachean Ethics* Bk. I, Ch.2.

III

THE GOLDEN AGE OF
RATIONALISM

A. RENE DESCARTES (1596–1650)

CARTESIAN DOUBT AND ITS RESOLUTION

Descartes is generally, and rightly, regarded as the pivotal figure in the transition from classical to modern philosophy. This is not so much a matter of the doctrines he put forward – a good many of which have now been questioned – as of his conception of philosophical inquiry. Descartes invented almost single-handed a striking and highly seductive picture of the method which the philosopher must pursue in his search for truth.

> Some years ago I was struck by the large number of falsehoods which I had accepted as true in my childhood, and by the highly doubtful nature of the whole edifice which I had subsequently based on them. I realised that it was necessary, once in the course of my life, to demolish everything completely and start again right from the foundations if I wanted to establish anything at all in the sciences that was stable and likely to last.[1]

This is the opening sentence of one of the most famous books in the history of philosophy, the *Meditations on First Philosophy*, published in Latin in 1641. The philosopher, in Descartes' conception, must start from scratch: he must systematically free himself from the accumulated presuppositions of the past and the preconceived opinions he has acquired from his parents and teachers.

The instrument for this clean sweep is the celebrated 'method of doubt': 'I resolved to reject as absolutely false anything in which I could imagine the least doubt, in order to see if I should not be left at the end with some belief that was absolutely indubitable.'[2] Descartes' doubt comes in three waves. First, the testimony of the senses is rejected: 'from time to time I have found that the senses deceive me, and it is prudent never to trust completely those who have deceived us even once.' Next, even judgements about present experience are rejected. The belief that 'I am sitting by the fire holding this piece of paper' seems at first sight the kind of judgement that is so straightforward that only a madman would doubt it; but it is possible that I may be dreaming, in which case my judgement is false. The scope of this argument (the 'dreaming argument' as it has come to be known) is extended to cast doubt on any judgement whatsoever which I may make about the external world; however, it does not impugn the truths of logic and mathematics, for, 'whether I am awake or asleep, two and three added together make five and a square has no more than four sides'. But now the third and most devastating wave of doubt arises. Suppose there is a deceiving God who systematically makes me go wrong whenever I add two and three or count the sides of a square. If there is such a 'malignant demon' – and I cannot so far disprove this possibility – then absolutely nothing seems free from doubt.[3]

But having pushed his method of doubt to its ultimate limits, Descartes now sees that there is at least one truth – one 'firm and immovable point' – which even the most extravagant scepticism cannot touch. If there is a deceiving demon then 'I too undoubtedly exist, if he is deceiving me. Let him deceive me as much as he can, he will never bring it about that I am nothing, so long as I think I am something.' Hence, '*I am, I exist* is, necessarily, true whenever it is put forward by me or conceived in my mind.'[4]

We have now arrived at the starting point of Descartes' philosophical system, the individual's knowledge of his own existence; the insight is elsewhere encapsulated in the famous dictum 'I am thinking, therefore I exist' (*je pense, donc je suis*, or, in Latin *cogito ergo sum*).[5] Having established his existence, Descartes now proceeds to investigate his nature or essence. What kind of thing am I? I am not essentially a physical being, for, applying the method of doubt, I can doubt whether I have a body – or indeed whether any external objects exist. The only attributes which I cannot deny of myself are mental ones, and hence I conclude that 'I am a substance whose whole nature or essence is to think and whose being requires no place and depends on no material thing.'[6]

Descartes' reconstruction of knowledge now begins to take off. He knows he exists; he knows he is essentially a thinking thing. Moreover, while he is aware of his own imperfections, he is also aware that he has within him the idea of a supremely perfect being. By a complex argument whose details may be omitted here, Descartes reasons that this idea must have been placed in him by a really existing perfect being – God. And, given the existence of a perfect, benevolent God who will not deceive him so long as he uses his reasoning powers carefully and methodically, the way is open to develop a systematic account of the workings of the physical world.

DESCARTES' CONCEPTION OF KNOWLEDGE; THE REJECTION OF THE SENSES

The first thing to strike the reader about Descartes' method of philosophizing is its highly individualistic stance. The meditator, alone by the fireside, attempts to rid himself of the prejudices of the past, and reflects on his own nature and existence. And at first sight this all seems far removed from the grand rationalistic design of Plato – the rejection of particularity, the assertion of an independently existing realm of impersonal, objective realities. But the more one looks at the details of the Cartesian philosophy, the more its profoundly rationalistic orientation emerges. To begin with, Descartes, like Plato, constantly insists that the mind must be 'led away from the senses' if true knowledge is to be achieved. This is partly because, as we have seen, our ordinary judgements about the external world are liable to error; sensory perceptions may be subject to error and illusion; indeed all our supposed observations might be delusions or dreams. But this is only half the story, and commentators who treat Descartes' arguments as simply following the path of conventional scepticism are leaving out something crucial. For even after the method of doubt has been left behind, Descartes continues to insist that our senses, even when they are in perfect working order, are still inherently unreliable informants about the true nature of reality. This comes out clearly in Descartes' discussions of our knowledge of the physical world; he gives the example of a piece of wax.

Let us take, for example, this piece of wax. It has just been taken from the honeycomb; it has not yet quite lost the taste of the honey; it retains some of the scent of the flowers from which it was gathered; its colour, shape and size are plain to see; it is hard, cold and can be handled without difficulty; if you rap it with your knuckle it emits a sound . . . But even as I speak, I put the wax by the fire and look: the residual taste is eliminated, the smell goes away, the colour changes, the shape is lost, the size increases; it becomes liquid and hot, and if you strike it it no longer emits a sound . . . So what was it in the wax which I understood with such distinctness? Evidently none of the properties arrived at by means of the senses.[7]

The ordinary sensible properties of the wax, Descartes asserts, tell us nothing about its essential nature. It emerges that the only essential property of the wax is its extension: it is simply a *res extensa*, an extended thing which has length, breadth and depth, and is capable of taking on an indefinite number of geometrical shapes. But this is not something we perceive via the senses or the imagination, for we know the wax is capable of taking on many more shapes than we can ever actually observe or picture to ourselves. Hence 'we know that bodies are not strictly perceived by the senses or by the faculty of imagination but by the intellect alone'.[8]

The key to this purely intellectual cognition is the *lux naturae* or 'light of nature': the innate capacity which God has implanted in our intellect for arriving at the truth by means of 'clear and distinct ideas'. These clear and distinct perceptions have nothing to do with the perceptions of the senses; instead they are the kind of purely intellectual perceptions that we enjoy when we are contemplating the elementary and self-evident propositions of mathematics. Indeed the properties of the wax which we clearly and distinctly perceive *are* mathematical, and, more specifically, geometrical properties: the wax is essentially something which is capable of being extended in three dimensions.

THE ROLE OF MATHEMATICS

The above point is of fundamental importance for the understanding of Cartesian physics. For Descartes conceives of the whole of knowledge as a systematic unity: 'philosophy is like a tree of which metaphysics forms the roots, physics the trunk, and the other sciences the branches.'[9] This means that the philosophical insights established in the *Meditations* are to be carried over into Descartes' detailed account of the physical universe. Our common-sense view of the world largely depends on our attributing sensible qualities to objects – qualities like hardness, colour, heaviness and so on. But Descartes insists that science has no place for such non-essential properties:

Suppose we attend to the idea we have of . . . a stone, and leave out everything we know to be non-essential to the nature of body. We will first of all exclude hardness since if the stone is melted or pulverized it will loose its hardness without thereby ceasing to be a body. Next we will exclude colour, since we have often seen stones so transparent as to lack colour. Next we will exclude heaviness, since although fire is extremely light it is still thought of as a body; and finally we will exclude cold, heat and all such qualities, either because they are not thought of as being in the stone, or because if they change the stone is not on that account reckoned to have lost the nature of a body. After all this we will see that nothing remains in the idea of the stone except that it is something extended in length, breadth and depth.[10]

The reasoning here is not entirely clear. If shape (a certain length, breadth and depth) is allowed to be a mode of

40

extension, why should not colour also be so regarded? If an object can be extended with a certain shape (so as to constitute, e.g. a square) why cannot it also be extended with a certain colour (so as to constitute, e.g. a yellow area)? Descartes' answer is that any mode of extension must be something *quantifiable*; for it is only the rigorously precise properties determined by mathematical reasoning which can be perceived so clearly and distinctly as to exclude all possibility of error. This emerges in Descartes' mammoth scientific-cum-philosophical treatise, the *Principles of Philosophy*, published in Latin in 1644:

> I freely acknowledge that I recognise no matter in corporeal things apart from that which the geometricians call quantity and take as the object of their demonstrations, i.e. that to whichevery kind of division, shape and motion is applicable. Moreover, I do not consider anything at all in matter apart from these divisions, shapes and motions; and even with regard to these I will admit as true only what has been derived from indubitable common notions [axioms] with such self-evidence that it is fit to be considered as a mathematical demonstration. And since all natural phenomena can be explained in this way, I do not think that any other principles are either admissible or desirable in physics.[11]

The Cartesian programme for the physical sciences is thus one of 'mathematicization'. Descartes proposes the systematic elimination of sensible qualities – together with obscure occult forces such as the sympathetic and antipathetic 'powers' or 'virtues' of medieval science – in favour of the strictly quantifiable properties of mathematical reasoning.

Descartes did not in actual fact succeed in producing a satisfactory mathematical model for the physical universe. The details of his theories on gravitation, the nature of fire, light, magnetism and the rest, are now of only historical interest, and it was left to Newton, later in the century,[12] to provide the precise mathematical equations that would give mankind for the first time a measure of real power to predict the course of nature. But for all that, Descartes' insistence that the route to progress must lie in a rationalist direction, via the clear and distinct perceptions of mathematical reasoning, has turned out to be substantially correct. And the programme for the elimination of *qualia* in favour of *quanta* – the search for explanations which avoid reference to sensible qualities and invoke only the precise quantitative descriptions of mathematics – remains one of the hallmarks of modern science.

PROBLEMS WITH DESCARTES' RATIONALISM

(i) The 'Cartesian circle'. There remain some important and awkward questions that need to be asked about Descartes' rationalist conception of knowledge. Firstly, the viability of the Cartesian enterprise – indeed its whole *raison d'être* – depends on getting the foundations right. Starting from scratch, casting aside all preconceived opinions, the Cartesian philosopher must be able to build up a systematic and indubitable system of clear and distinct perceptions. But how can this be done? Descartes' method, as we have seen, depends on proceeding from knowledge of one's own existence to knowledge of the existence of a non-deceiving God. So if the proofs of God's existence are invalid, as most critics now agree that they are, then of course the whole enterprise collapses. But the problem is not just a matter of the doubtful validity of Descartes' proofs for the existence of God: there is a more serious structural worry underlying the whole enterprise. In order to set about proving God's existence we must start from certain premises or axioms. But how do we know these axioms are correct? The answer which Descartes gives us is that we clearly and distinctly perceive their truth. But now the question arises: how can we trust our clear and distinct perceptions? Once God's existence has been proved, this is no problem. For Descartes can claim that God, being perfect and hence benevolent, cannot have given us a mind that is subject to error on matters which it thinks it perceives with the utmost clarity. But until we know that God exists, we have, it seems, no guarantee of the reliability of the mind even on the simplest points. A sinister circularity thus seems to threaten the

Cartesian enterprise from the beginning: we cannot trust our clear and distinct perceptions until we know that God exists; but we cannot prove God exists without relying on our clear and distinct perceptions.

Descartes' answer to this notorious problem (which is known as the 'Cartesian circle') appears to be that there are some propositions which are so clear and simple that, even without any divine guarantee of the reliability of the mind, they are self-guaranteeing. 'Two plus two equals four' or 'if I think, I exist' are such simple and straightforward propositions that, so long as I attend to what they assert, I cannot possibly be mistaken as to their truth.[13] Philosophers are divided as to whether this notion of the indubitably true, self-guaranteeing proposition is a coherent one; but it seems to the present writer that it is. Propositions of the sort just cited are indeed assertions such that, so long as I attend to the meanings of the symbols involved, I can infallibly know them to be true. The difficulty for Descartes, however, is that such tautologous or near-tautologous propositions give us very little information: they do not go beyond relatively uninformative assertions about the meanings of our symbols or the contents of our own mind. But as soon as we want to go further – as soon as we want to establish more substantial claims about the existence of God or the nature of the universe – then it seems that we are bound to move beyond the realm of elementary, self-confirming propositions, and the infallible guarantee of truth will therefore vanish.

The rationalist project of pure philosophical inquiry on which Descartes is engaged thus seems to face a fatal dilemma. Either it begins and ends with thin and unexciting propositions such as 'two plus two equals four' or 'if I am thinking, I exist', which buy their truth at the cost of being relatively uninformative; or else it advances to more important and substantive truths at the cost of losing the kind of certainty and necessity which was originally demanded as an absolute requirement for a well-founded system of knowledge.

(ii) The limitations of the senses. A second difficulty with the Cartesian method concerns Descartes' reason for rejecting the senses as a reliable source of information about the world. It is certainly true, as Descartes frequently observes, that many of the propositions established by sensory observation fail to be true immutably and for all time: the wax is now hard, now soft. But why does this show that empirical observation is an unreliable basis for knowledge? Because a property is *contingent*, present or absent depending on varying conditions and circumstances, why should this make it any less true and genuine a property of the object in question? We seem here to be up against the Platonic prejudice described in the previous chapter – the prejudice that only eternal and immutable properties can qualify as material for true knowledge. But even if we accept the Platonic view, it is still not clear that the information of the senses should be ruled out of court. The property 'hard' is indeed a fleeting and transitory property of the wax; but the property 'hard at ten degrees Celsius' is an eternal and unchanging one. In other words, there seems to be no reason why the senses cannot give us reliable and stable information about the nature of things, provided we are careful to specify the conditions for their application.

(iii) Mathematics and science. Thirdly, and lastly, problems arise with Descartes' aprioristic conception of scientific method. Like Plato (and Aristotle), Descartes wants his philosophy to uncover immutable and eternal verities about the universe. But it seems doubtful whether the deductive certainties of mathematics can do the work that is expected of them here. Descartes firmly states his deductivist aspirations in his famous *Discourse* (*Discourse on the Method of rightly conducting one's Reason and seeking Truth in the Sciences* published in French in 1637 and intended as a popular introduction to his work). The statement we find is in many ways paradigmatic for the entire rationalist enterprise:

Those long chains of very simple and easy arguments geometricians customarily use to arrive at their most difficult demonstrations gave me the idea that everything that can fall under human knowledge forms a similar sequence; and that so long as we avoid accepting as true what is not so, and always preserve the right order for deducing one thing from another, there can be nothing too remote to be reached in the end or too well hidden to be discovered.[14]

The parallel with geometry has led to the standard complaint that the rationalist is trying to do science from the armchair. For while the step-by-step deduction from first principles may be spectacularly successful in geometry, where the aim is to unfold the consequences of a selected set of axioms, it seems that physics must do very much more than this. It must tell us not merely what follows from what, but what the world is actually like. To put it another way, the principles of physics must describe, or at least somehow map on to, what in fact occurs. And here it seems that it will simply not do to rely on our *a priori* intuitions; for why should we suppose that our intuitions reflect the actual structure of the universe?

Part of Descartes' answer is to have recourse to the notion of innate knowledge. The *lux naturae*, the divine light of reason which God has implanted in each of us, is, when used carefully and reflectively, an infallible guide to the nature of reality. One trouble with this is the problem of circularity already discussed: if the proofs of God's existence presuppose the reliability of the natural light, then the existence of a non-deceiving God cannot without circularity be used to establish that the human mind is a reliable instrument for discovering the truth. But even if we grant Descartes his 'natural light', it seems highly optimistic to hope that the kinds of simple and self-evident propositions which we know *a priori* will be rich and detailed enough to describe the complexities of the actual universe. The rationalist philosopher begins here to look like Bacon's spider[15] – spinning elaborate metaphysical webs which may have a certain internal fascination, but which may well not bear any useful relation to the real world.

DESCARTES' CONCEPTION OF SCIENTIFIC INQUIRY

Some of Descartes' scientific work (e.g. his attempts to derive the laws of motion *a priori* from the nature of God) are undoubtedly ammunition for those who dismiss the rationalist enterprise as 'armchair science'. But elsewhere Descartes proposes a much less rigid model. Even in his early work, the *Rules for the Direction of the Understanding*, which lays great stress on mathematical intuition, Descartes roundly attacks the scholastic philosophers for neglecting experiments and 'expecting truth to germinate from their own heads like Minerva from the head of Jupiter'.[16] And in the *Discourse*, Descartes is adamant that 'the progress of science makes experiment more and more necessary'. He goes on to say:

the power of nature is so ample and vast, and my principles so simple and general, that, for any particular effect that I observe, I know straightaway that there are many different ways in which it can be deduced from the principles ... Here I know of no other expedient than to look for further experiments that will give different results, depending on whether one or another explanation is correct.[17]

This certainly does not seem to be rigid apriorism. And if one looks at Descartes' detailed scientific results, it turns out that only very few quite general principles are put forward as demonstrable *a priori*. For the rest, Descartes says, 'we are free to make any assumption consistent with our principles provided all the consequences which follow from it square with experience.'[18] Instead of 'armchair science', this looks much more like the standard modern conception of a 'hypothetico-deductive' conception of science: a theory is advanced and its deducible consequences checked against experience.

It seems in the end that science is, for Descartes, a two-level process. At the first level, our *a priori* intuitions must be used to construct a set of fundamental first principles which provide a basis for a precise mathematical description of the laws of nature. But at this level of generality almost all the specific details still remain to be filled in. To provide the detail we must descend to a lower level, where something much closer to a hypothetico-deductive approach operates. Here the aim is to devise hypotheses of maximum simplicity which will be judged in terms of the scope and diversity of the actual observational results which they are capable of explaining. This is a complex and sophisticated model for scientific theory, and if it is 'rationalism' then rationalism may well turn out to be something which science cannot do without.

B. BENEDICTUS DE SPINOZA (1632–77)

THE DEDUCTIVE METHOD

We have seen how the deductive model of knowledge played a crucial role in Descartes' thinking. But, interestingly enough, the way in which Descartes actually expounded his philosophical system was not, in the main, deductive. He certainly believed that his metaphysics conformed to the canons of deductive certainty – indeed its truth and indubitability depended on just that. But in order to take his readers with him, Descartes avoided the formal axiomatic style of exposition and preferred to employ instead what he called the 'order of discovery'.[19] Thus in the *Meditations* he does not deduce conclusions from a set of initial axioms but instead dramatically describes the route taken by the individual thinker in his escape from doubt and his gradual progress to the truth. Only once, to please his friend and critic Mersenne, did Descartes attempt to expound his system '*more geometrico*' – in geometrical fashion – starting from a set of definitions, axioms and postulates, and deducing his results as theorems. But the presentation is brief and schematic, and Descartes himself does not seem to have been especially pleased with it.[20]

Spinoza, however, is the deductivist *par excellence*. The definitive statement of his philosophy is the *Ethica ordine geometrico demonstrata* ('Ethics demonstrated in geometrical order'), written in Latin in the 1660s but not published until 1677, just after his death. Here Spinoza sets out an entire philosophical system in strictly deductive fashion, along the lines of Euclid's *Geometry*. Definitions are listed, axioms are laid down, and then a large number of 'propositions' and 'corollaries' are demonstrated, with each stage in the reasoning being justified by showing that it follows in a precise step-by-step fashion from the definitions and axioms.

As the title suggests, Spinoza's object is to give an account of the good for man, and in the latter parts of the work we find a detailed account of human passions and emotions and of the nature of freedom. But the first and best known part of the work constructs a metaphysical theory of the universe from first principles, beginning with what is for Spinoza the most fundamental notion, that of *substance*.

THE MONISTIC THEORY OF SUBSTANCE

The philosophical notion of substance comes from Aristotle, where it is used primarily to apply to that which is a subject of predication, but which cannot be predicated of other things: thus, whiteness is not a substance but a predicate applied to other things; but an individual horse or man is a substance.[21] Scholastic medieval philosophy follows Aristotle in treating the world as a plurality of substances which fall under various 'natural kinds'; but in Descartes there are just two kinds of substance – mind (or thinking substance) and matter (or extended substance). Spinoza simplifies things still further and maintains that there is, necessarily, only one substance. Definition III of the *Ethics* lays it down that 'a substance is that which is in itself and is conceived through itself; in other words, that of which a conception can be formed independently of any other conception'. It follows from this that a substance is a self-sufficient and independent entity which is *causa sui* – the cause of its own existence; for if it were caused by something else, it could not be conceived entirely 'through itself' and hence would not qualify as a substance as originally defined. (Though Spinoza is about to depart radically from the Aristotelian account, his definition owes something to the original Aristotelian conception of substance; for Aristotle had suggested that a substance, being an ultimate subject of predication, is, therefore, something which has independent existence.[22]) Now to explain or understand a substance is, for Spinoza, to conceive of it in terms of its essential or necessary properties (here we see a strong link with the rationalism of Plato and Descartes: true explanations must be explanations not in terms of accidental or contingent properties but in terms of immutable, necessary properties). Suppose, then, that there were two substances. If this were so, then in order to provide an explanation of their essential nature, we should have to explain how they were related (or unrelated). But such an explanation would necessarily mean that we would have to look beyond the essential properties of each substance; yet in that case the objects in question could not be substances (for, by the original definition, to qualify as a substance an object must be self-sufficient, conceived 'in itself and through itself'). It follows, given Spinoza's initial premises, that there can be only one substance, which is independent, immutable, infinite, the cause of itself, and which necessarily and eternally exists.

Spinoza's metaphysical 'monism', as it is aptly called, thus presents us with an enclosed and unified system in which the entire universe with all its complexities is a manifestation of one single reality. This unity has an infinite number of attributes, and these, says Spinoza, can be conceived sometimes as modes of extension or physical modes, and sometimes as modes of thought or mental modes. But these apparently diverse phenomena are in reality merely aspects of the one single self-determining and all inclusive substance, which Spinoza labels *Deus sive Natura* – 'God or Nature'.[23]

TRUTH AS COHERENCE

There is no space here to do justice to the complexity and detail of Spinoza's derivation of his results. But some of the problems with this highly aprioristic philosophical system will already be apparent from our earlier discussion of Descartes. The type of rigorous certainty that Spinoza, following Descartes, insists upon leads him inexorably to a deductive conception of knowledge where all the results can be shown to follow inevitably and logically from the first principles of the system. But, as with all rationalist systems, it is appropriate to ask what warrant we have for supposing that the system, for all its internal rigour and clarity, corresponds to what the real universe is actually like. Some critics have accused Spinoza of perpetrating a kind of gigantic conjuring trick: proposition after proposition rolls out of his deductive machinery, but if the initial assumptions are questioned the whole system will collapse like a house of cards. Though there is some justification for this complaint, it can be argued in Spinoza's defence that his enterprise should not be judged solely in terms of the plausibility of the initial postulates. Rather, it is intended to function as what is nowadays called a *holistic* system: the axioms and original definitions can be understood only in terms of the propositions which are subsequently deduced, while the subsequent deductions have to be referred back to the axioms and definitions. This system must be assessed not piecemeal, but as an entirety.

The implications of this defence of Spinoza are complicated and they depend in part on our conception of truth. The empiricist tradition tends to analyse truth as a matter of *correspondence* with reality: the universe consists of such and such entities, or works in such and such a way, and a statement is true only if it corresponds with the facts – with the way things actually are. Seen in this light, the Spinozian system seems to offer us little or no evidence that it has uncovered the true characteristics of the universe. But there is an alternative conception of truth, which has had a powerful revival in our own century, according to which the truth of a proposition is to be analysed not in terms of its correspondence with the facts, but in terms of the *coherence* which it has with the total system of assertions with which it belongs. Such coherence theories reject the notion that we can somehow determine whether a given proposition does or does not correspond with the extra-linguistic 'facts'. For one thing, it may not be possible to specify the meaning of a proposition in isolation; its significance can only be understood in terms of its function in the language and the way in which it fits in with other elements of the system. And in the second place, the idea that we can somehow step outside our conceptual scheme and compare our assertions with 'reality' to see if they 'fit' seems on reflection to be a notion which it is hard to make sense of.

It is beyond the scope of this volume to evaluate the highly complex issues involved in the debate between the correspondence and the coherence theories of truth. But it is interesting to note that Spinoza himself develops the basis for a coherence account of truth in the *Ethics*. Spinoza's conception of truth hinges on what he calls an 'adequate idea'. To say of an idea that it is adequate is to say that it stands in a certain logical relation to other ideas, which means, ultimately, that it can be demonstrated to have a necessary connection with the system as a whole. Truth is thus what Spinoza calls an 'intrinsic' rather than an 'extrinsic' property; and he specifically rejects the analysis of the truth of an idea in terms of its correspondence with an external object. 'I talk of the intrinsic mark of an adequate idea in order to exclude that which is extrinsic, namely the agreement or correspondence (*convenientia*) between the idea and its object.'[24]

THE HOLISTIC THEORY OF EXPLANATION

Spinoza's coherence theory of truth is bound up with his holistic account of explanation. In a letter to Henry Oldenburg he asserts that 'each part of nature agrees with the whole'. And he goes on to illustrate his meaning by means of an imaginary example of 'a little worm living in the blood and able to distinguish by sight the particles of the blood, lymph, etc.', and to observe the way in which each particle reacts with every other particle. Such a worm, Spinoza asserts, 'would live in the blood in the same way as we live in a part of the universe'. But if the worm confined himself to an individual and piecemeal examination of his environment, 'he would be unable to determine how all the parts are modified by the general nature of the blood and are compelled by it to adapt themselves so as to stand in a fixed relation to one another.'[25] In short, we must grasp the system as a whole before we can satisfactorily explain the behaviour of the parts. This passage reveals one important contrast between the rationalism of Spinoza and that of Descartes. For Descartes, scientific explanation is essentially *reductionist*: the diverse phenomena which make up the universe can all be reduced to, or explained in terms of, the mechanical interaction of particles of matter whose shapes, sizes and motions can be mathematically quantified. For Spinoza, the direction of explanation is reversed: any given action or reaction, however precisely and mathematically described, can be fully accounted for only in terms of its relation to the structure of the universe as a whole.

MIND AND BODY

One issue which provides a crucial test case for Spinozan holism is the relation between mind and body. First, a word about the background to Spinoza's position. For Plato, the human soul is immortal and essentially separable from the physical realm of change and decay; it cannot be affected by the collapse or destruction of the body.[26] Descartes preserves this Platonic doctrine but develops and refines it in terms of a 'real distinction' between two radically different kinds of substance, mind and matter. The mind is a *res cogitans*, a thinking substance, which is essentially indivisible and unextended; it does not occupy space and depends on no material thing. Matter, by contrast, is defined in terms of exactly opposite essential features: it is *res extensa*, extended and therefore essentially divisible substance, which by its nature must always occupy space. Hence mind and body are not only different but fundamentally opposed and incompatible kinds of substance.[27] Now, given this incompatibility, a serious problem arises for Descartes – one which he frequently wrestled with, but which he never was able to accommodate satisfactorily within his system. The problem is that, as we all know from our own common experience, mind and body frequently interact. When there is a physical change in the body (e.g. my leg is damaged), there is a corresponding mental change (I feel pain); and, conversely, when there is a mental change (e.g. I decide to raise my hand), a physical change follows (my arm goes up). As Hume later ironically observed, 'is there any principle in all nature more mysterious than the union of soul and body by which a supposed spiritual substance acquires such an influence over a material one that the most refined thought is able to actuate the grossest matter? Were we empowered, by a secret wish, to remove mountains or control planets in their orbit, this extensive authority would not be more extraordinary, nor more beyond our comprehension.'[28] One could, of course, merely accept it as a brute fact that such interaction occurs: we just do have this power over our bodies, and our bodies just do affect our mental states. But this will not do for the rationalist, since his whole enterprise requires that whatever occurs should be clearly and distinctly intelligible in terms of strictly necessary connections. Descartes himself was driven to admit that such clarity and distinctness is simply not obtainable when it comes to the relation between mind and body: we experience in our everyday sensations (like hunger and thirst) a kind of 'substantial union' between mind and matter; but our perception of it is obscure and confused.[29]

The rationalist disciples of Descartes were led to some desperate expedients in their attempts to solve this problem. Nicolas Malebranche (1638–1715), accepting that by the logic of the Cartesian position there can be no interaction between the two logically distinct substances of mind and matter, developed the curious theory known as 'occasionalism', according to which God miraculously intervenes so as to cause my arm to go up whenever I decide to raise it.[30] This seems less of an explanation than an admission that the relation between mind and body is an inexplicable mystery. Spinoza, however, makes the remarkable and original move of preserving Descartes' rationalism while rejecting his dualism. Indeed, rationalism for Spinoza entails that dualism must be false; for if dualism were true there would be an arbitrary and unexplained relation between mind and body, and this would be incompatible with the rationalist claim that there are clear and rationally intelligible links connecting all phenomena. Spinoza's own solution is that 'the order and connection between ideas is the same as the order and connection of things'. Or, quite simply, 'mind and body are one and the same thing'.[31] It is true, Spinoza admits, that we can conceive of the one substance, God or Nature, in either one of two different ways: we can conceive of substance 'under the attribute of thought' (as a mind), or we can conceive of it 'under the attribute of extension' (as matter). But 'whether we conceive of nature under the attribute of thought or under the attribute of extension we shall find the same order or one and the same chain of causes, that is the same things following in either case'.[32] Spinoza goes on to develop this notion in terms of his doctrine of the 'infinite attributes' of God. Just as the infinite mode of extension covers all that is physical, so the infinite mode of intellect covers all that can be thought.

THE RELATION BETWEEN PSYCHOLOGY AND PHYSIOLOGY

Some critics have found Spinoza's account of mind and body distinctly enigmatic. Has Spinoza really succeeded in side-stepping the snares of Cartesian dualism, or does not the talk of attributes in effect reintroduce the two Cartesian realms of mind and matter in another guise? For if the 'attributes' are indeed fundamentally different (and they do seem to involve radically different kinds of property) then how can Spinoza baldly assert that they relate to the single substance?

In a letter to Simon de Vries of 1663, Spinoza took this up. His correspondent had asked him 'to illustrate by an example how one and the same thing can be stamped with two different names'. Spinoza uses an example from the Old Testament. The name 'Israel' is used to refer to a certain individual; but this individual is elsewhere referred to by a different name 'Jacob'. Yet the two names designate the same person – the Third Patriarch.[33] What Spinoza seems to be saying here is that the fact that there are two labels should not lead us to suppose that there are two separate substances which are mysteriously linked. Rather, there is one single subject of which different attributes are true, just as, in the example, whatever is true of Jacob is true of Israel, and vice versa. The example is too cursory to be philosophically satisfying. But it is interesting to see how many modern philosophers have begun to approach the mind in terms of the Spinozian model of a single entity describable in different ways. Current 'attributive' theories of the mind assert that when I say 'S is in pain', I am referring, by means of a 'mentalistic' or psychological description, to the self-same events that can also be referred to using a physiological description of the workings of S's brain. There are two sets of descriptions but only one set of occurrences. It must be said, however, that supporters of this theory are still a very long way from explaining exactly *how* a series of electrical and chemical impulses in the brain can somehow constitute, or be an alternative description of, a psychological experience like having a pain or a colour-sensation; for such experiences have a specific quality, accessible only to the subject having them, and this makes it hard to see how mentalistic language can be simply an alternative way of describing neuro-physiological events.[34] Thus, even if it is true that mental phenomena are simply physical phenomena under a different description, the rationalist programme for explaining exactly how the mental descriptions are related to the physical descriptions remains largely unfulfilled.

SPINOZA'S NECESSITARIANISM

In unravelling Spinoza's system we have so far focused on three main strands: his deductivism, his holistic account of truth and explanation, and his metaphysical monism. Before we end our discussion we need to mention one further element, which is in fact closely bound up with all the others. This is what is commonly called Spinoza's 'necessitarianism'. One of the initial axioms of the *Ethics* is that 'from a given definite cause an effect necessarily follows'.[35] This claim, as we shall see, was to be a prime target of Hume's critique of rationalism. But Spinoza goes further than asserting that causes necessitate their effects: he denies that the universe contains any contingent (non-necessary) events whatsoever. 'Nothing in the universe is contingent, but all things are conditioned to exist and operate in a particular manner by the necessity of the divine nature.'[36] This follows directly from Spinoza's monism. For whatever exists is an aspect of the one substance that is God. And since that substance is necessarily self-caused and self-determining, all its attributes must necessarily follow from its essence or nature. Hence 'all things are conditioned by the necessity of the divine nature not only to exist but also to exist and operate in a particular manner, and there is nothing that is contingent'.[37]

To say that an event 'E' is *necessary* is to exclude the

possibility of 'not-E'; in other words, it is to say that 'E' cannot be otherwise. This obviously has important implications for the idea of human freedom, for it is a widely held belief (and one shared by many philosophers) that we act freely when and only when we *could have done otherwise*. Spinoza attacks this notion, and suggests that our conception of ourselves as undetermined agents is false.

An infant believes that of its own will it desires milk and an angry child believes that it freely desires vengeance ... But experience tells us clearly that men believe themselves to be free simply because they are conscious of their actions and unconscious of the causes whereby these actions are determined; further, it is plain that the dictates of the mind are simply another name for the appetites that vary according to the varying state of the body.[38]

The connection with Spinoza's monism is again evident here. All events, whether described as mental or physical, are merely aspects of one and the same universally determined totality. As Spinoza puts it: 'A mental decision and bodily determined state are . . . one and the same which we call decision when it is regarded under the attribute of thought, and a conditioned state when it is regarded under the attribute of extension and deduced from the laws of motion and rest.'[39]

In spite of this thoroughgoing determinism, Spinoza did none the less attempt to show that at least some human beings have a measure of individual freedom. Each individual, says Spinoza, has an internal principle or power of striving – what Spinoza calls *conatus*: 'the power or endeavour whereby each thing endeavours to persist in its own being.'[40] By expressing our own natures and resisting external forces, we can become free. Such self-expression involves, for Spinoza, a process of rational adjustment whereby, through the exercise of reason, we may control and master our passions and find our true selves. It was left to Leibniz, however, to attempt to provide a detailed reconciliation between the belief in human freedom and the tenets of a thoroughgoing rationalist framework of universally determined causes.

C. GOTTFRIED WILHELM LEIBNIZ
(1646–1716)

Leibniz, like Descartes and Spinoza, aimed to construct a coherent and all-embracing philosophical account of the universe. And as with his predecessors, the notion of substance lies at the centre of the system. But whereas for Descartes there are two categories of substance, and for Spinoza only one, Leibniz reverts to the older and more commonsensical Aristotelian view that there is a plurality of substances. Leibniz' inquiry can be seen as starting from an analysis of the ordinary ways in which we talk about the world. Whenever we make an assertion about the world we make a statement of the form 'so and so is such and such'; that is, we ascribe some attribute or property to some subject. A question then arises as to the nature of these subjects: what *are* the underlying entities or substances to which the various attributes are applied said to 'belong'? As Leibniz expresses it, 'since actions and passions properly belong to individual substances, it will be necessary to explain what such a substance is.'[41]

The inquiry, then, is closely bound up with the logical structure of ordinary statements (or propositions). Indeed for Bertrand Russell (one of whose earliest publications was a critique of Leibniz' philosophy) Leibniz' metaphysics is 'almost entirely derived from his logic'.[42] (By 'logic' here, Russell meant the analysis of the proposition and its truth.) Russell's interpretation, as will emerge, puts too little emphasis on the place of God in Leibniz' system. But in approaching Leibniz' metaphysics, it is none the less helpful to start with an examination of his doctrines concerning the proposition.

TRUTHS OF REASON AND TRUTHS OF FACT

Leibniz divided all true propositions into two classes, viz., truths of reason (*vérités de raison*) and truths of fact (*vérités de fait*). He defines these classes as follows: 'Truths of reason are those which are necessary and of which the opposite is impossible, and truths of fact are those which are contingent and of which the opposite is possible.'[43]

This crucial distinction between propositions which have to be and those which happen to be true has played a vital part in modern philosophy; though it is the work of Kant (centring on his dual distinction between the analytic and synthetic on the one hand, and the *a priori* and *a posteriori* on the other) that has been historically more influential. In fact however, Leibniz' *method* of drawing the distinction between his two types of proposition is reminiscent in many ways of Kant's later account of analyticity (to be discussed in the following chapter) even though the two philosophers differ widely as to precisely *where* the line is to be drawn. But Leibniz' account presents some special problems of its own.

The account of truths of reason is simple enough. Leibniz derives these from his 'Principle of Contradiction' – one of the two great principles on which he claims our reasoning is founded.[44] This principle says simply that a proposition is true if its opposite (by which is meant its negation or contradictory) implies a contradiction. Thus, to call something a triangle but to deny that it was three-sided would be to contradict oneself; hence 'all triangles are three-sided' is a truth of reason. Putting it another way, Leibniz says that the reasons for the truth of such propositions can be found through *analysis*, since they either are, or can be reduced by analysis to, 'identical propositions'. These identical propositions are what we should call tautologies – propositions of the form 'A is A'. To take the triangle example again, our proposition 'all triangles are three-sided' can be converted by means of the definitional equivalence 'triangle = three-sided figure' to the proposition 'all three-sided figures are three-sided': that is, it can be reduced by analysis to a tautology. Incidentally, it is interesting to note in this connection that Leibniz regarded the propositions of mathematics as essentially tautological,[45] thus going against the later analysis of Kant, but anticipating the view of many modern thinkers.

Leibniz' view of contingent propositions is more idiosyn-
cratic and more complicated. Leibniz aimed to avoid the
universal necessitarianism of Spinoza, and find a place for
contingent truths with his system. But a major problem
arises when Leibniz puts forward his famous doctrine that
for all true propositions the predicate is contained in the
subject (*praedicatum inest subiecto*).[46] Leibniz expressed this
(in a letter to Antoine Arnauld) as follows: 'Always, in
every true affirmative proposition, whether necessary or
contingent, universal or particular, the concept of the
predicate is in some way comprehended in that of the
subject, *praedicatum inest subiecto*; otherwise I know not what
truth is.'[47]

Now this is very strange. The notion of the subject
'comprehending' or 'containing' the predicate, though
somewhat metaphorical, is perhaps intelligible enough, and
was taken over by Kant. But for Kant, the feature of the
predicate's being contained within the subject was confined
to – indeed was the hallmark of – the *analytic* proposition.
And this is what we should expect. If we take our old
example – 'All triangles are three-sided' – it seems plausible
to say that the necessary truth of this proposition derives
from the fact that the concept of three-sidedness is contained within the concept of triangularity; the one concept
is logically bound up with the other. But what of a
particular contingent proposition, like 'Ronald Reagan was
elected President in 1980'? To say that the concept of
winning the 1980 election is contained within the subject
here seems to suggest that there is some inevitable link
between being Ronald Reagan and winning the election.
But this is precisely what one would want to deny: Reagan
did *in fact* win the election, but he *might* not have done. At
this stage, the doctrine that, in *all* true propositions, the
predicate is contained within the subject not only appears
intuitively bizarre, but, worse, threatens to blur the very
distinction between truths of reason and truths of fact that
Leibniz is so anxious to articulate.

THE MONADS

Before we discuss whether Leibniz was able to find a way out of this difficulty, let us go back and see how the doctrine of containedness described above ties in with Leibniz' inquiries about substance and his theory of monads. The connection is in fact explicitly made by Leibniz. In the *Discourse on Metaphysics* (written in French in 1686), after referring to the doctrine that the subject must always contain the predicate, Leibniz goes on to say: 'This being so we can say that the nature of an individual substance or of a complete being is to have a notion so complete that it is sufficient to comprise and to allow the deduction from it of all the predicates of the subject . . .'[48]

Leibniz then uses the example of Alexander the Great, and says that if one were able to perceive the 'thisness' (or 'haecceity') of Alexander, one would be able to see the foundation and reason of everything that can truly be said of him (e.g. that he would conquer Darius). Thus, every individual substance has 'inside it', so to speak, everything that it has ever done or will do. We have now arrived at the metaphysical counterpart of the doctrine *'praedicatum inest subiecto'*, namely the doctrine of the monad: the individual unit of substance, 'laden with its past and pregnant with its future', containing once and for all everything that has ever happened or will ever happen to it.

The theory of monads laden with internal properties may seem somewhat quaint to the modern reader, and may appear to be of only historical interest. But one current issue on which the theory perhaps has something relevant to say is that of the nature of scientific explanation. The empiricist account of science is based on the notion of observed correlations (what Hume called 'constant conjunctions') between different phenomena. The rationalist view, by contrast, insists that such brute correlations can never provide satisfactory explanations of what occurs: they may describe *what* we observe, but they can never explain *why* the objects around us behave as they do. To arrive at a more satisfying explanation the rationalist argues that we must look beneath the observed correlations to an investigation of the internal structural properties of matter – properties which will tell us not just that matter *does* behave in such and such a way, but which will explain why it *must* so behave. This thesis that scientific explanation must be sought in terms of essential properties or fundamental inner structures thus owes at least something to the Leibnizian theory of substance. The point will become clearer when we turn to the closely connected Leibnizian Principle of Sufficient Reason.

Having argued that his monads are 'complete' (contain within themselves all their predicates) Leibniz goes on to demonstrate that they must be 'self-contained' or 'changeless', in the sense that they do not need to be acted upon externally in order to change. In the famous Leibnizian metaphor, they are 'windowless' – they work completely independently of each other.[49]

The theory of complete, self-contained individual substances that has now emerged presents Leibniz with two major problems. First, how, if the monads are truly self-contained, is Leibniz to explain the apparent causal connections we observe around us – the fact that the things in our world seem to act and react upon one another in a regular fashion? The second problem is the difficulty referred to already: how, if the monads are truly complete (contain once and for all everything that will happen to them), is Leibniz to preserve the contingent character of the class of truths of fact? Significantly enough, the resolution of both these problems takes us straight into Leibnizian theology, and depends heavily on the existence of the Supreme Monad – God.

CAUSAL INTERACTION

Leibniz solves the problem of causal interaction by means of his theory of Pre-Established Harmony. God, in creating the universe, brought it about that all the monads should independently work together so as to form the most perfect whole. Thus, though no monad has windows, each monad is, as it were, a mirror of the universe. 'This connection of all created things with every single one of them and their adaptation to every single one', writes Leibniz, 'has the result that every single substance stands in relations which express all the others. Whence every single substance is a perpetual living mirror of the universe.'[50]

A special case of the problem of the interaction of substances, which enables Leibniz to make full use of his principle of Pre-Established Harmony, is the problem of the relationship of mind and body. The absolute Cartesian distinction between mind and matter tends to be rejected in Leibniz' system; for there is a sense in which all the monads possess a germ of consciousness in so far as they individually mirror the whole universe. But, in another sense, the monad which constitutes a given human soul is logically quite distinct from, and independent of, the set of monads that constitute the corresponding body. Leibniz' way out of this complex maze is to regard the body as a sort of automaton, which God (with complete foreknow-ledge of our intentions) has programmed in advance, according to the system of Pre-Established Harmony, to perform the acts willed by the soul.[51] This 'solution' is perhaps unlikely to be very satisfying to the modern philosopher of mind; but Leibniz clearly regarded it as an advance on the more fantastic 'occasionalism' of his prede-cessors.[52]

THE PROBLEM OF CONTINGENCY AND THE PRINCIPLE OF SUFFICIENT REASON

Leibniz attempts to elucidate the status of contingent truth in his system by means of his famous Principle of Sufficient Reason. We have seen that necessary truths are true in virtue of the Principle of Contradiction. But there is also, Leibniz asserts, a Principle of Sufficient Reason '. . . by virtue of which we hold that no fact can be true or existing . . . without a sufficient reason for its being so and no different; albeit these reasons must most frequently remain unknown to us.'[53]

The concluding qualification here has led some interpreters to construe the Principle of Sufficient Reason as a methodological postulate: as scientists we must assume that there is an explanation to be found somewhere for everything that occurs. This interpretation squares well with Leibniz' assertion of a Principle of Continuity – the principle that 'Nature never makes leaps'. But Leibniz means more than this by his Principle of Sufficient Reason. For Leibniz, everything that happens in the world originates in the creative act of the Supreme Monad. Contingent truth is thus considered in the light of God's original act of choice in creating our universe: 'Since in the divine ideas there is an infinity of possible universes of which only one can exist, the choice made by God must have a sufficient reason which determines him to the one rather than to the other. This reason can only be found in fitness, that is, in the degree of perfection contained in these worlds.'[54]

Thus, God having chosen our world from all possible worlds as the most perfect, it follows that a 'reason' for any event in the world can, in principle, be found in terms of the original selection made by God. Any given particular substance behaves in this way, rather than some other way, because of its place as a member of the total set of substances necessary to build the most perfect universe. As Leibniz puts it: 'God, legislating for the whole, has considered every part, and particularly every monad.'[55]

It does not of course follow from this that human scientists can, or will ever be able to, discover sufficient reasons for any particular contingent truth. An investigation of the reason for any particular event would, says Leibniz, involve us in a complex and infinite chain of causes.[56] It belongs only to God to perceive the sufficient reason behind every event. But what Leibniz does want to assert is that behind each event there is, whether we can discover it or not, a rationally intelligible reason why it occurs in the way it does, and not in some other way. Here we have one of the most fundamental and important tenets of rationalism – the assertion that the universe contains no 'brute facts' – no arbitrary correlations which just happen to occur.

It may well be asked, however, whether Leibniz' Principle of Sufficient Reason really does anything to elucidate the dubious status of contingent truth in his system. For the picture of the universe that begins to emerge is one in which every true statement could (at least by an infinite intelligence) be deduced *a priori*, in which each single substance contains inside itself once and for all the germ of all it will do. Does it not follow from this that every true proposition is in some sense necessary? Leibniz himself felt the pressure of this sort of difficulty, and felt it most acutely in the area of human action, where his metaphysical scheme raised the thorny problem of the Freedom of the Will. He writes, in connection with his theory of substance: 'It seems that this will destroy the difference between contingent and necessary truths, and that human liberty will have no more place, and that an absolute fate will reign over all our actions as well as over all the other events in the world.'[57]

Although this was written as early as 1686, Leibniz was to become increasingly concerned with the moral and theological problems arising out of his system.

FREEDOM AND NECESSITY

As a defender of Christian theism, Leibniz was committed to the doctrines of personal responsibility and desert, and therefore to finding a place in his philosophical system for human freedom. But, precisely because of the character of the rest of his system, this turns out to be a major task. The problem is this: if the monad that constitutes, for example, Julius Caesar, has once and for all 'built into it', the attribute 'crosser of the Rubicon' (this predicate being, like all the others, contained in the subject), how can it be said of Julius Caesar that he freely chose to cross the Rubicon? For, under Leibniz' schema, the decision was necessarily 'part of him'. Leibniz' answer (the example is his own) is that it was logically possible that Caesar should not have crossed the Rubicon; hence there was no necessity about his decision to cross the river; for 'nothing is necessary of which the opposite is possible'.[58] The suggestion here is clearly that 'Caesar crossed the Rubicon' is a 'truth of fact', not a 'truth of reason': to say 'Caesar did not cross the Rubicon' is not to contradict oneself. But unfortunately this answer merely glosses over the difficulty. For if God chose the universe which was the best and most perfect of all possible universes, and Julius Caesar (together with all his attributes) is a constituent of the universe that God in fact selected as being the most perfect, then it is hard to see how Caesar's decision was in any meaningful sense open, or 'up to him'. The mere possibility that God might have selected another universe in which there was a deutero-Caesar who did not cross the Rubicon is hardly enough to bestow any genuine freedom or avoidability on Julius Caesar's actual decision.

Leibniz returned to these problems in detail in the longest work which he published, the *Theodicy*, subtitled 'Essays on the Goodness of God, the Freedom of Man, and the Origin of Evil'. The contributions here to the problem of freedom are interesting in that they anticipate the work of many modern 'Reconciliationists' – philosophers who attempt to find a place for the notion of human freedom within the framework of a thoroughgoing scientific determinism. Leibniz himself, as a logical result of his system of monads and Pre-Established Harmony, is, like Spinoza, a convinced determinist: 'All is certain and determined beforehand in man, as everywhere else,' he writes, 'and the human soul is a kind of spiritual automaton.'[59] To hold that freedom was possible within this completely determined universe represented a clean break with the Cartesian insistence on the unlimited and undetermined power of human choice. 'M. Descartes', writes Leibniz 'demands a freedom which is not needed, by his insistence that the actions of the will of man are altogether undetermined, a thing which never happens.'[60]

Leibniz' reconciliationist defence of freedom hinges on the

notion of *spontaneity*: 'there is a marvellous spontaneity which in a certain sense makes the soul in its resolves independent of the physical influence of any other creatures.'[61] Leibniz is clearly thinking here of the self-containedness of the monads, which are not subject to external constraints, but all work independently, though in concert, through the system of Pre-Established Harmony. The Leibnizian suggestion is thus that if my choices are independent and undetermined by outside forces, then my resulting actions are free. For if I choose something because I spontaneously want it, then what, it may be asked, can be freer than that? This analysis of freedom as the absence of external constraint has been highly influential, but it does not, in the end, appear to do the job required to reconcile Leibniz' determinism with the existence of free will. For to be free in the sense required for full human autonomy and responsibility, it does not seem sufficient that my decisions are my own spontaneous choices, unconstrained by external forces. What is surely needed in addition is that I have genuine alternative options which I could have taken; and this, as we have seen in the case of Caesar and his decision to cross the Rubicon, seems to be ruled out in Leibniz' system. Leibniz elsewhere admits that we are bound to act the way we do, given that a motive of a particular strength is a part of our character, but he goes on to claim that motives 'incline without necessitating'.[62] All that this apparently comes down to, however, is that there is a logically possible world in which any given decision of mine was not in fact taken. But this merely takes us back to the unsatisfactory move made by Leibniz in the case of Caesar and the Rubicon. The mere *logical* possibility of an alternative decision in an alternative universe does not show that a given person on a given occasion could in fact have decided otherwise than he did. The upshot is that, despite his valiant attempt to defend the notions of contingency and human freedom, Leibniz is always in danger of allowing his system to slip down the Spinozan path to universal necessitarianism.

The three great seventeenth-century rationalists are remarkable for the power and scope of their vision of philosophy and its ability to uncover necessary truths about the universe. But the very notion of necessity which arises so often in their systems was shortly to become the focus of a remarkable analysis by David Hume which threatened to undermine the entire rationalist enterprise. For Hume was to argue that we have no meaningful concept of necessity apart from the purely formal notion of necessity used in logic, and hence that it makes no sense to claim that we can uncover supposedly necessary connections operating in the real world. Hume's critique of rationalism, and the philosophical developments that led up to it, will be one of the major topics of our next chapter.

NOTES

1. *Meditations* (1641) [31] VII, 17; [33] I,144.
2. From the *Discourse on the Method* (1637) [31] VI, 34; [33] I, 101.
3. *First Meditation,* [31] VII, 21; [33] I, 147.
4. *Second Meditation* [31] VII, 25; [33] I, 150.
5. *Discourse* [31] VI, 33; [33] I, 102.
6. *Ibid*.
7. *Second Meditation* [31] VII, 30; [33] I, 154.
8. *Ibid*. VII, 34; [33] I, 155.
9. *Principles of Philosophy,* Preface to first French edition (1647); [31] IXb, 14; [33] I, 211.
10. *Principles of Philosophy* (1644) Part II, Art. 11 [31] VIII, 46; [33] I, 259.
11. *Ibid*. Part II, Art. 64 [31] VIII, 79.
12. Newton's *Principles (Philosophiae Naturalis Principia Mathematica)* were published in 1687.
13. *Conversation with Burman* (1648) [35] pp.xxixff. and p.6.
14. *Discourse* [31] VI, 19; [33] I, 92.
15. See above, Ch.I, p.7.
16. *Rules* [31] X,380; [33] I, 15.
17. *Discourse* [31] VI, 64/5; [33] I, 121.
18. *Principles* Part III, Art. 46 [31] VIII, 101. For more on Descartes' conception of scientific inquiry see Clarke, *Descartes' Philosophy of Science* [39].
19. *Conversation with Burman* [35] p.69; [31] V, 152–3.
20. *Second Replies* (1641) [31] VII, 160ff; for Descartes' attitude see VII, 159; cf. [33] II, 51ff.

21. *Categories* 2 a 12 [22] [23].
22. *Ibid.* 1 a 24/5 and 2 a 13.
23. *Ethics* Part I Prop.29; Part II Props.1, 2, 7 [43] [44].
24. *Ibid.* Part II Def. IV.
25. Letter 32 in Elwes, *The Chief Works of Benedict de Spinoza* [44] Vol.II, p.291.
26. Cf. *Republic* Bk.X.
27. Cf. *Sixth Meditation*.
28. *Enquiry concerning Human Understanding* (1748) [73] Section VII, Part I.
29. Cf. *Sixth Meditation* [31] VII 81; and letter to Elizabeth of 28 June 1643 [31] III, 690ff.
30. *Recherche de la Vérité* (1674), Preface.
31. *Ethics* Part II Prop. 7.
32. *Ibid.*
33. Letter IX (Elwes [44] p.316.).
34. Cf. Nagel, 'What is it like to be a bat?' in *Mortal Questions* [51].
35. *Ethics* Part I Axiom III.
36. *Ibid.* Prop. 29.
37. *Ibid.*
38. *Ibid.*, Part III Prop. 4.
39. *Ibid.*
40. *Ibid.*, Prop. 7.
41. *Discourse on Metaphysics* (1686) VII [56].
42. Russell, *A Critical Exposition of the Philosophy of Leibniz* [64]. See Preface to second edition.
43. *Monadology* (1714) [57] para.33.
44. *Ibid.*, para. 31.
45. *Ibid.*, paras. 34/5.
46. This needs qualification: Leibniz held that the idea of existence (which he regards as a predicate) is normally *not* contained in the subject. The sole exception concerns the concept of God which for Leibniz (as for Descartes and Spinoza) necessarily involves that of existence.
47. Letter of July 1686 in *The Leibniz-Arnauld Correspondence* [59] p.63.
48. *Discourse on Metaphysics*, VIII [56].
49. *Monadology*, para.7.
50. *Ibid.*, para.56.
51. *Theodicy* (1710) [58] Part I, para. 66.
52. See above p.54.
53. *Monadology*, para. 32.
54. *Ibid.*, 53, 4.
55. *Ibid.*, 60.
56. *Ibid.*, 36.

57. *Discourse on Metaphysics*, XIII.
58. *Ibid.*
59. *Theodicy*, Part I, para. 59.
60. *Ibid.*; *Preliminary Dissertation on the Conformity of Faith and Reason*, para. 69. There are, however, passages in Descartes where the approach to freedom seems closer to that of Leibnitz; Cf. *Fourth Meditation*, [31] VII, 59.
61. *Theodicy*, Part I, para. 59.
62. *Ibid.*, 43. Cf. Parkinson, *Leibniz on Human Freedom* [66].

IV

THE EMPIRICIST
COUNTER-REVOLUTION AND
THE KANTIAN SYNTHESIS

A. LOCKE'S CRITIQUE OF INNATE IDEAS

One of the cornerstones of the rationalist edifice of *a priori* knowledge is the notion that the mind is furnished from birth with certain fundamental principles or ideas; these 'innate ideas' are the basis from which the rationalists claimed to construct their metaphysical systems independently (to a greater or lesser extent) of the senses. As we have seen, the theory of innateness plays an important role in the thought of Plato, while for Descartes the whole enterprise of pure philosophical inquiry depends on the innate *lux naturae* – the 'light of nature' which enables us to reject the misleading evidence of the senses and uncover the essential structure of reality. Descartes did not deny that some of our ideas (those which he called 'adventitious' ideas) come from the senses: our idea of the sun as a luminous yellow body roughly equal in size to the moon, is, says Descartes, derived largely from sensory observation. But such ideas can provide little or no information about the true nature of things. If we want to know how things really are, we must concentrate not on sensory impressions but on more fundamental notions such as extension and number, which form the basis for our 'clear and distinct perceptions' – and these notions are innate. Such notions include 'the idea of God, mind, body, a triangle and in general all ideas which represent true and immutable essences'.[1]

At the end of the seventeenth century the theory of innate ideas was subjected to the most searching scrutiny by the English philosopher John Locke (1632–1704), whose *Essay*

Concerning Human Understanding (1690) is one of the most influential texts in the history of philosophy. The object of the *Essay* is nothing less than 'to inquire into the original, certainty and extent of human knowledge',[2] and its central conclusion is that all knowledge springs from experience. Locke mounts his uncompromising attack on the innateness doctrine in the first few pages of Book I of the *Essay*:

> It is an established opinion amongst some men that there are in the understanding certain *innate principles*, some primary notions . . . characters as it were stamped upon the mind of man, which the soul receives at its very first being, and brings into the world with it. It would be sufficient to convince unprejudiced readers of the falseness of this supposition if I could only show (as I hope I shall in the following parts of this Discourse) how men . . . may attain to all the knowledge they have without the help of any innate impressions . . .[3]

UNIVERSAL ASSENT AND AWARENESS

Locke's strategy in rejecting the theory of innate ideas has a negative and a positive side. On the negative side he argues that none of the arguments normally employed to support the theory are adequate. The argument most commonly used by innatists is the 'argument from universal assent': there are certain fundamental principles which all mankind accepts as true. But universal assent, Locke objects, proves nothing. If universal assent is the mark of innateness, then a proposition such as 'white is not black' would have to be considered innate. Yet 'no proposition can be innate unless the ideas about which it is be innate'; and it would be absurd to say that our ideas of 'white' and 'black' are innate, since we obviously get them from having *seen* white and black objects.[4] But in any case, Locke goes on to argue, the premise that the supposedly innate principles command universal assent is not even true: 'these propositions are so far from having a universal assent that there are a great part of mankind to whom they are not so much as known.'[5] Some people (Locke cites the case of 'idiots and children') are unaware even of the simplest of these principles: they have not 'the least apprehension or thought of them'. And if we consider some of the more abstract principles of logic and mathematics, then it seems that the majority of the human race go through their lives without ever being aware of them at all. The innatist may reply here that though 'the mass of mankind' never explicitly formulate such principles they are at least *implicitly* aware of them. But Locke now acutely asks what such talk of 'implicit awareness' really amounts to. The innatist's claim is supposed to be that these truths are imprinted on the mind from birth; but what can it mean to say that a truth is 'imprinted' if the mind is not in actual fact consciously aware of it? It is of course true that all normally endowed humans can, given suitable training, come to recognize the truth of principles like the law of non-contradiction, or mathematical propositions about squares such as the one which Socrates was able to get the slave boy to see in the *Meno*.[6] But the fact that humans have the capacity to become aware of such truths hardly supports the innateness hypothesis, as Locke vigorously points out.

If the *capacity* for knowing be the natural [innate] impression contended for, all the truths a man ever comes to know will, by this account, be every one of them innate; and this great point will amount to no more [than] a very improper way of speaking which, whilst it pretends to assert the contrary says nothing different from those who deny innate principles. For nobody, I think, ever denied that the mind was capable of knowing several truths.[7]

THE MIND AS '*TABULA RASA*'

The positive side of Locke's strategy is to show that all the categories of knowledge which the rationalist attributes to innate ideas can be shown to be acquired through experience. The mind at birth is a *tabula rasa* – a 'white paper void of all characters':

How, then comes the mind to be furnished? Whence comes it by that vast store which the busy and boundless fancy of man has painted on it with an almost endless variety? Whence has it all the materials of reason and knowledge? To this I answer, in one word, from *experience*. In that all our knowledge is founded, and from that it ultimately derives itself.[8]

Here is as straightforward a statement of the empiricist outlook as one could wish for. All knowledge is ultimately derived from experience; and experience, for Locke, consists principally in *sensation* – the direct awareness of the world around us which the mind has by means of the five senses. In addition to the ideas of sensation, Locke allows that there are ideas of 'reflection' – ideas which occur when the mind reflects on its own operations, and compares and organizes its sensory impressions;[9] but the ultimate building blocks for all knowledge are sensory impressions. This account dismisses at a stroke not just the doctrine of innateness, but also the entire rationalist programme for transcending the world of the senses and establishing the nature of reality by reason alone. David Hume, writing some fifty years after Locke, was to press this point home with great force. Any genuine and meaningful human idea must ultimately be based on some sense-impression: 'when we entertain . . . any suspicion that a philosophical term is employed without any meaning or idea (as is but too frequent) we need but enquire *from what impression is that supposed idea derived*? And if it be impossible to assign any, this will serve to confirm our suspicion.'[10]

To both Locke and Hume it seemed so obvious as to be hardly worth arguing that without the stimulation of the senses, the mind would be blind – empty of all concepts whatsoever. 'It will be granted easily', says Locke, 'that if a child were kept in a place where he never saw any other [colour] but black and white till he were a man, he would have no more ideas of scarlet and green than he that from his childhood never tasted an oyster, or a pineapple, has of those particular relishes'.[11] It is perhaps rather unfair of Locke to use as examples such obviously sensory ideas as those of colours and tastes; but the argument can be extended to cover all ideas, even the logical and mathematical ideas on which the innatists rely. For whatever the subject matter, it seems that the mind must initially have *some* sensory input in order, as it were, to 'get going'; otherwise it would surely remain utterly empty and undeveloped.

Contemporaries of Descartes had already raised this type of objection to the Cartesian doctrine of innateness. Could the mind really operate in the absence of all sensory stimuli? Does the mind of the infant, for example, really meditate on metaphysics in its mother's womb? Remarkably, Descartes seems prepared to bite the bullet and accept this consequence of his theory. He does partly cover himself by suggesting that the infant may not have time to concentrate on metaphysics because it is constantly bombarded with bodily stimuli, but he insists that 'nonetheless it has in itself the ideas of God, and all such truths are called self-evident . . .; it does not acquire these ideas later on as it grows older. I have no doubt that if it were taken out of the prison of the body, it would find them within itself.'[12]

LEIBNIZ' REPLY TO LOCKE

Descartes' answer seems too fanciful, too much a violation of common sense, to be very plausible. But some of the later rationalists proposed a less extreme version of the innateness theory which avoids some of these difficulties. Leibniz, whose *Nouveaux Essais sur l'entendement humain* (*c.* 1704), was intended as a reply to Locke's *Essay*, concedes that sensory stimulation is *necessary* if the mind is to develop. But such stimulation, Leibniz urges, is not *sufficient* for the acquisition of knowledge. Sense perception may elicit knowledge, but only in so far as it enables us to see what is already 'hidden within us, but appearing at the instance of the senses like the sparks which come from the steel when it strikes the flint'.[13] In order to support this view, Leibniz cites the propositions of logic and mathematics. These subjects deal with necessary and eternal truths – propositions whose verification is quite independent of experience. No number of instances or experiments can, for example, establish the truth of an Euclidian theorem: the proofs are purely deductive and *a priori*.

To the Lockean objection that such truths can hardly be 'implanted' or 'imprinted' in the mind from birth, since young children for example are quite unaware of their truth, Leibniz replies that 'we must not imagine that we can read the eternal laws of reason in the soul as in an open book'.[14] The eternal verities are present in the mind not in a fully developed form but as dispositions or '*virtualités*'. To elucidate this, Leibniz suggestively compares the human mind to a sculptor's block of marble – not a uniform block indifferently suited to receive any shape the sculptor may choose to impose upon it, but a block already *veined* in a particular pattern, so that the sculptor has only to chip away and uncover the vein in order to reveal the shape underneath.[15] Thus knowledge arises, for Leibniz, out of a combination of sensory stimuli (the blows of the sculptor) and an innate set of 'natural inclinations, dispositions, habits or powers' of the mind. He sums up his position by adding to the empiricist slogan '*nihil est in intellectus quod non prius fuerit in sensu*' ('there is nothing in the intellect which was not previously in the senses') the crucial qualification '*excipe: nisi ipse intellectus*' ('except the mind itself').[16]

Leibniz has here put his finger on one of the central defects in the empiricist conception of knowledge. For Locke, the mind is essentially a passive receptor: 'in the reception of simple Ideas the Understanding is for the most part passive'.[17] But this, as Leibniz points out, fails to do justice to the active role played by the mind in its perception of the environment. No theory of knowledge is adequate unless it allows for the contribution made by the mind itself ('*ipse intellectus*') in organizing and processing the sensory inputs. As we shall shortly see, this idea was to play a crucial role in Kant's synthesis between empiricism and rationalism. And in our own day, the distinguished philosopher and linguistic scientist Noam Chomsky has followed Leibniz in rejecting the passive empiricist conception of the mind and insisting on the importance of pre-existing mental structures (in Chomsky's case these innate structures are invoked in order to explain certain facts about the way in which language is acquired).[18]

B. DAVID HUME AND THE IDEA OF NECESSARY CONNECTION

It is in the philosophy of the Scottish philosopher David Hume (1711–1776) that the British empiricist movement of the seventeenth and eighteenth centuries finds its most sophisticated expression, and the attack on the aspirations of the rationalists reaches its climax. In *A Treatise of Human Nature* (1739–40) Hume begins his investigations with an analysis of the origins of our ideas (the empiricists followed Descartes in using the term 'idea' to refer to any mental content of which we are directly aware). Hume accepts Locke's thesis that all our ideas are ultimately derived from experience; the contents of the mind consist either of the directly apprehended sense-data (which Hume calls 'impressions'), or derivative ideas such as those of memory which are copies of original impressions ('all our simple ideas in their first appearance are derived from simple impressions which . . . they exactly represent').[19]

RELATIONS OF IDEAS AND MATTERS OF FACT

In the *Enquiry concerning Human Understanding* (1748) (which was intended as a clearer and more accessible restatement of the main doctrines of the *Treatise*) Hume divides all the objects of human reason into two basic categories: 'relations of ideas' and 'matters of fact'. Relations of ideas – Hume gives as examples arithmetical propositions such as 'twice fifteen is thirty' – are truths 'discoverable by the mere operation of thought'; but, as their name implies, they simply express internal relationships between our concepts (thus 'twice fifteen is thirty' simply asserts that a relation of equivalence holds between the concept of 'twice fifteen' and the concept of 'thirty'). To deny such propositions is self-contradictory; they are, in modern philosophical jargon, 'tautologies'. And tautologies, although they have the highest degree of certainty, do not depend on, or provide information about, anything which actually exists in the universe. Matters of fact, on the other hand, relate to what actually exists in the world. Because they make substantive claims about the world their denial is always possible; thus '*that the sun will not rise tomorrow* is no less intelligible a proposition and implies no more contradiction than the affirmation *that it will rise*'.[20] Pure logic, then, cannot establish the truth of matters of fact; and Hume now proceeds to take his uncompromising stand against the rationalists: 'I shall venture to affirm, as a general proposition, which admits of no exception, that the knowledge [of matters of fact] is not, in any instance, attained by reasonings *a priori*; but arises entirely from experience'.[21] The upshot is that human understanding can never take us beyond, on the one hand, the uninformative tautologies of logic and mathematics, and, on the other hand, experiential claims which must be based on empirical observation:

When we run over our libraries, persuaded of these principles, what havoc must we make? If we take in our hand any volume; of divinity or school metaphysics, for instance; let us ask, *Does it contain any abstract reasoning concerning quantity or number?* No. *Does it contain any experimental reasoning concerning matter of fact and existence?* No. Commit it then to the flames: for it can contain nothing but sophistry and illusion.[22]

This famous conclusion, with its ruthless dismissal of the claims of rationalism to transcend the realm of sensory experience, encapsulates the essence of empiricist philosophy; and, as we shall see in our final chapter, it became the battle cry for the logical positivist movement of the mid-twentieth century which rejected as quite meaningless any assertion which was not either tautologous or empirically verifiable.

CAUSALITY

A large part of both the *Treatise* and the *Enquiry concerning Human Understanding* is taken up with a detailed analysis of what Hume takes to be the central and fundamental type of inference which human beings employ when dealing with matters of fact, namely *causal* inference: 'all reasonings concerning matter of fact seem to be founded on the relation of *Cause and Effect*.[23] But what does this relation really amount to? What do we mean when we say that the heat *causes* water to boil, or that the application of a mixture of nitric and hydrochloric acid *causes* gold to dissolve? Hume argues in the *Treatise* that when we say A is the cause of B the relationship between A and B breaks down into three elements, namely *priority*, *contiguity* and *necessary connection*. If A causes B then, firstly, A must be prior in time to B (since no effect can precede its cause). Secondly, A must be in contact with B (it is not however clear that this second condition is in fact required: the moon, for example, can cause changes in the tides without being in contact with them; and mental causes, e.g. desires, do not seem to be contiguous with their effects, e.g. decisions – a consideration that later led Hume to abandon the contiguity requirement). Thirdly, and most importantly, people believe that there is some necessary connection between cause and effect: if we believe A causes B, then we believe that A somehow 'makes' B happen, or that, given A, B is 'bound' to occur, or that given A, B 'must' follow.

Hume now turns his formidable powers of analysis on this notion of necessity. What can it mean to say that a piece of coal *must* when placed on a red hot fire? The 'must', Hume rightly argues, cannot be a *logical* 'must'. There is no logical necessity about the coal igniting: it is not a logical contradiction to assert that it will not burn (in the way that it is, for example, a logical contradiction to say that twice fifteen is not thirty, or that a bachelor is married). But if not from logic, then whence does our idea of causal necessity arise? Not, Hume insists, from observation. There is nothing that we actually observe that corresponds to the idea of necessity; we have no sensory impression of the supposed 'force', 'efficacy' or 'productive power' of causes. All that we actually observe, and this is the crux of Hume's position, is a certain repetition or regularity in events. Whenever the piece of coal has been placed on the fire, we have observed it burn. But that is all. There is no empirical justification or warrant for any further idea of 'necessity': it is not derived from any sensory impression.

Having reached this disquieting result, Hume now delivers his final devastating thrust. The idea of 'causal necessity', so far from corresponding to anything actually existing in the world, is simply something which arises in the mind as a result of the habitual expectations set up by repeated past observations. All we really observe is a series of correlations between events of type A and events of type B; and it is this constant conjunction between As and Bs that leads us to impose some real necessity on events when there is none really there.

> When one particular species of event has always in all instances, been conjoined with another . . . we call the one object *Cause*; the other, *Effect*. We suppose that there is some connection between them; some power in the one, by which it infallibly produces the other . . . This idea of a necessary connection among events arises from . . . the constant conjunction of these events . . . After a repetition of similar instances, the mind is carried by habit upon the appearance of one event, to expect its usual attendent . . . This connection, therefore, which we *feel* in the mind . . . is the sentiment or impression from which we form the idea of necessary connection. Nothing farther is in the case.[24]

Hume's revolutionary conclusion is thus that there *are* no necessary causal connections in the world. There are merely repetitions of events which arouse certain habitual expectations in the mind, thus producing in us a feeling of inevitability which we mistakenly foist on the real world.

PROBLEMS WITH THE HUMEAN ACCOUNT

The Humean account of causation presents a number of difficulties. For one thing, the psychological thesis which Hume uses to underpin his attack on the concept of real necessity seems to be suspect. If Hume's thesis were correct, then wherever we observed a repeated conjunction of As with Bs, we should, without more ado, call A the cause and B the effect. But causal inferences are more than the automatically induced expectations of Pavlov's dogs (conditioned by constant repetitions to expect their food whenever the bell rings). No matter how often As are followed by Bs, we do not always automatically say that A *causes* B; to take a famous example,[25] if two clocks run perpetually together so that whenever clock A ticks, clock B ticks, we should never, even after a billion repetitions, say that clock A's ticking *causes* B to tick. In order for a causal link to be posited, we normally require that the events in question should fit into some overall pattern which coheres with the rest of our scientific theory. Thus dampness may be accepted as the cause of my car's not starting, since this explanation fits in with theoretical laws of physics and chemistry but the singing of a robin, no matter how often it preceded my car's failure to start, would never be accepted as the cause.

There are also problems with Hume's claim that causal relations are nothing more than constant conjunctions. Hume himself, having defined cause as '*an object followed by another, and where all the objects similar to the first are followed by objects similar to the second*', goes on to add 'or, in other words, *where if the object had not been, the second never had existed*'.[26] But the added clause is very far from being simply a restatement ('in other words') of the initial definition in terms of constant conjunction. The initial definition simply states that all actual instances of A are followed by instances of B (e.g. 'whenever the temperature is lowered, the water turns to ice'); but the additional clause involves a contrary-to-fact conditional in the subjunctive mood; that is, it asserts that B *would not* have occurred if (contrary to fact) A *had not* occurred (ice *would not* have formed had the temperature not been lowered). Such contrary-to-fact conditionals by their very nature take us beyond the realm of what is or was in actual fact the case. This is not to say that Hume was wrong to add the extra clause. For the counterfactual claim does indeed seem to be a crucial part of what we mean when we say that A causes B (our reason for not allowing that clock A causes clock B to tick in the above example is precisely that we suppose that clock B *would have* continued to tick even if clock A *had not* existed). But the problem for Hume is that if counterfactual statements are implied by causal statements (and they surely are), then it seems that causal statements are more than simple statements about conjunctions of actual events.

Despite these problems, Hume's influence on subsequent philosophical thought has been enormous, and there are many philosophers today who believe that his account can be salvaged, and that the regularity view of causation is essentially correct.[27] For our purposes, however, the crucial importance of Hume's account of causation is the sceptical challenge which it offers to the claims of the rationalists. Descartes' theory of clear and distinct ideas and Leibniz' principle of sufficient reason had held out the hope that philosophical reason could uncover the eternal necessary connections underlying all reality. Hume's challenge to the rationalists is that they must explain what precisely this alleged 'necessity' can consist in. If the supposedly necessary connections are supposed to be established *a priori*, then the Humean objection will be that the only truths which can be established in this way are the essentially uninformative tautologies of logic and mathematics. And if the necessary connections are supposed to be confirmed *a posteriori*, by experience, then the Humean critic will object that no actual empirical observation that can be produced will establish anything more than a mere contingent regularity. It was this challenge which was to rouse Immanuel Kant (1724–1804) from his 'dogmatic slumbers' and to lead him to construct his original and highly complex account of the nature and limits of human reason.

C. THE KANTIAN SYNTHESIS

When Kant began teaching at the University of Konigsberg in 1755, the prevailing philosophy of the German 'Enlightenment' was firmly rationalist in character. The thought of Leibniz had been erected into an elaborate metaphysical system by Christian Wolff (1679–1754) and further extended and developed by Wolff's pupil Alexander Baumgarten (1714–62). Kant's greatest work *The Critique of Pure Reason (Kritik der Reinen Vernunft*, 1781) arose out of the tensions between this rationalist orthodoxy and the empiricist scepticism of Hume with respect to causal necessity and *a priori* knowledge. It was Hume's account of causation that, in Kant's own words, 'first interrupted my dogmatic slumbers and gave a completely different direction to my inquiries in the field of speculative theory'.[28]

ANALYTIC AND SYNTHETIC; SYNTHETIC *A PRIORI* JUDGEMENTS

First, a word about terminology, and in particular about Kant's classification of judgements, which remains a standard tool of philosophical analysis today. Firstly, Kant distinguishes between *a priori* and *a posteriori* judgements (this distinction has a long philosophical history and is derived ultimately from Aristotle). An *a posteriori* judgement (based on ordinary observation) deals with routine contingent truths such as 'the cat is sitting on the mat'. *A priori* judgements (such as those of mathematics) are by contrast both *necessary* and *universal* ('they have strict universality in such a manner that no exception is allowed to be possible'.[29]) In addition to this distinction, Kant introduces a distinction of his own between *analytic* and *synthetic* judgements. Analytic judgements (such as 'bachelors are unmarried') are judgements where, as Kant puts it, the predicate is *contained* within the subject (thus the concept of being unmarried is contained within the concept of being a bachelor). A synthetic judgement, on the other hand, takes us beyond the realm of tautologies and gives us substantive information about the world. Thus 'all bachelors are under eight foot tall' is a synthetic judgement (the property of being under eight foot tall is not contained within the concept of being a bachelor).

If the empiricist position is presented in terms of this pair of distinctions, then it is very straightforward: the two distinctions exactly coincide. All *a priori* truths are analytic: they are merely what Hume called 'relations between ideas'; their universality and necessity arises solely from their being tautologies. Similarly, all synthetic truths, all propositions which give real information about the world, are, for the empiricist, arrived at *a posteriori* – by observation; and such truths are never necessary but are always purely contingent (they might be otherwise, and at any given moment they may cease to be true). Kant however makes his crucial departure from the empiricists when he claims that there are genuine *synthetic a priori* judgements. That is, there are propositions which supply information about the world but whose truth is none the less *a priori*, universal and necessary. Kant in fact argues that mathematical propositions are of this kind (a claim later to be hotly disputed by the logical positivists who insisted that the truths of arithmetic and geometry are simply elaborate tautologies). But, for our purposes, Kant's most important example of a synthetic *a priori* judgement is the law of causation – 'every event has a cause' or, as Kant puts it, 'every change occurs in accordance with the law of the connection of cause and effect'.[30] This proposition is not, says Kant, analytic, for the concept of a change does not logically imply the idea of something which is caused. But it is none the less a universally and necessarily true proposition which can be proved by human reason. One of the fundamental aims of *The Critique of Pure Reason* is to show how such 'synthetic *a priori*' judgements are possible.

THE LIMITS OF REASON

The title '*Critique of Pure Reason*' initially suggests an anti-rationalist stance, and indeed in the second part of the book (the so-called 'Dialectic'), Kant aims to deflate the pretensions of rationalist metaphysics to provide us with knowledge of ultimate reality. The only possible objects of knowledge, Kant asserts, are *phenomena* – the empirically observable objects of the physical world. 'Nothing is really given us save perception and the empirical advance from this to other possible perceptions.'[31] We cannot possibly arrive at knowledge of an ultimate world of 'noumena' – things as they are 'in themselves', apart from any perspective of the knower. Any attempt to transcend the limits of sense-experience leads inescapably to 'antinomies' – paradoxes and contradictions. Kant thus firmly resists the rationalist project of 'pure inquiry' – the attempt to ascend beyond the medium of experience to some supposedly 'absolute' world of unconditional knowledge. Such rationalist pretensions are condemned by Kant in a famous metaphor: 'the light dove, cleaving the air in her free flight, might imagine that flight would be easier still in empty space.'[32] Such aspirations are fruitless; there is no possible description of the world that can free itself from some reference to experience.

EXPERIENCE AND THE 'CONCEPTS OF THE UNDERSTANDING'

Though sceptical of the rationalist enterprise, Kant is equally critical of the empiricist view, put forward by Locke and Hume, that sense-impressions by themselves serve as the basis for knowledge. The idea that the mind experiences the environment by passively receiving impressions from the senses is dismissed by Kant as absurd. Mere raw sensation cannot be the basis for understanding anything; Kant insists, following Leibniz,[33] that the active power of the mind must be involved if even the simplest sensation is to be processed and understood. In experiencing the world, the mind necessarily interprets it in terms of a certain structure; it approaches the world already armed with what Kant calls 'concepts of the understanding' (*Verstandesb egriffe*). To approach the world without such concepts would not be to *experience* at all, but merely to have a kind of immediate sensory awareness which Kant calls 'intuition' (*Anschauung*). This is not to deny that sense-impressions are necessary in order to give content to our experience – on this point the empiricists were right. A mind without sensory data would be a mind without contents – a mind with nothing to think about. Kant thus asserts that there is an important grain of truth in both the empiricist and the rationalist approaches to knowledge, and he sums this up in the famous dictum 'thoughts without content are empty; intuitions without concepts are blind'.[34] The Lockean and the Leibnizian positions are thus both flawed: 'Leibniz *intellectualised* appearances just as Locke . . . *sensualised* all concepts of the understanding.' In reality, our intellectual and sensory faculties 'can supply objectively valid judgements of things only in conjunction with each other'.[35]

If the mind, in order to experience the world, must already be armed with 'concepts', where do these concepts come from and, more important, how can we establish that they have the kind of objective validity necessary to constitute knowledge? This is the central problem of the *Critique*. Kant's answer is that all the concepts of the understanding are derived from certain fundamental 'categories' (a term borrowed from Aristotle's metaphysics). These categories of the understanding, such as the category of substance and the category of causality are, Kant asserts, *a priori* notions; and in this sense the Kantian theory of the categories may be seen as following the traditional rationalist doctrine of innate ideas. But in contrast to the Cartesian view that these ideas are wholly independent of sensory experience, Kant argues – and this is his most crucial and original contribution to the theory of knowledge – that they are *presupposed* by experience. Categories such as those of substance and causality are necessary preconditions for our being able to experience the world at all. If the world is to appear to us in the way that it does, indeed, if we are to have any apprehension of the world at all, then our apprehension must conform to these categories:

The objective validity of the categories as *a priori* concepts rests on the fact that, so far as the form of thought is concerned, through them alone does experience become possible. They relate of necessity and *a priori* to experience, for the reason that only by means of them can any object whatsoever of experience be thought.[36]

Kant called this approach to knowledge his 'Copernican revolution'. Just as Copernicus explained the diurnal motions of the sun and stars by suggesting that it was the earthly spectator, not the sun and stars, which revolved, so Kant suggests that our knowledge of the world should be approached not by starting from the supposed properties of 'things in themselves', but by starting from the structure imposed by the understanding itself. However, although Kant was extremely proud of his 'revolution', it is not at first sight clear that it is as innovative as he supposed. As we have seen, Hume made precisely such a 'Copernican' move by analysing the concept of causal necessity not in terms of a real connection existing between objects in the world, but in terms of the propensity of the *mind* to impose its own subjective feelings of inevitability on reality. Moreover, this comparison with Hume's strategy raises crucial doubts about the validity of Kant's procedure. For the thrust of the Humean strategy is profoundly sceptical and destructive: there *is* no real necessity in the world; there are only purely contingent correlations. The mind has an automatic tendency to 'spread itself on external objects'[37] but the feeling of necessity arises solely from the promptings of the mind: 'nothing farther is the case.'

THE TRANSCENDENTAL DEDUCTION; KANT ON CAUSALITY

Kant was adamant in rejecting what he called this 'merely subjective' ('*bloss-subjektiv*') account of necessity. Our causal judgements, he insists, are 'necessary and in the strongest sense universal *a priori* judgements'.[38] But to make this claim good, he has the task of establishing that the 'categories' are not merely subjective aspects of our thought, but have 'objective validity'.[39] In order to do this, Kant developed a highly complex barrage of arguments which he calls the 'Transcendental Deduction' of the categories. In the case of causation, Kant sets out to prove, as a universal *a priori* necessary truth, that 'all changes occur in accordance with the law of cause and effect'. The proof is long and detailed, but it proceeds somewhat as follows. When I perceive an object (e.g. a house), the order of my perceptions is reversible: I can observe the roof first, then the basement, but I can equally well observe these elements the other way round. But when I perceive an *event* (e.g. a boat sailing down the river), the appearances are not similarly reversible: I can only experience the various elements in a particular order. Now this order is not subjective: it belongs to the appearances themselves, not to my apprehension of them. Hence, in the perception of an event, there is always a rule which makes the order of the perceptions *necessary* (*'diese Regel is bei der Wahrnehmung von dem was geschiet jederzeit anzutreffen, und sie macht die Ordnung der einander folgenden Wahrnemungen* notwendig').[40] This already implies, according to Kant, that there is something wrong with the Humean account of causation. On the Humean view, it is through repeatedly observing B following A that we discover a regularity which gives rise to our idea of causation. But on Kant's argument we would not be able to recognize the complex 'A, then B' as an *event* in the first place, unless there were a rule that makes it necessary that the order of our perceptions should be thus and not otherwise. In short, the very experience of an external event already presupposes an understanding of causal necessity.

If Kant's argument is correct (and the details of his proof are still the subject of philosophical debate), then we can break through the scepticism of the empiricists and achieve necessary *a priori* knowledge of the structure of the world. However, the 'synthetic *a priori*' law that every event is determined by a cause is true only in so far as it relates to the empirical world of phenomena – the world of 'appearances'. This is the essence of the remarkable Kantian synthesis between empiricism and rationalism. On the one hand there is the possibility of objective, *a priori* knowledge; the empiricist picture which limits us to passive reception of data and allows no real necessities beyond our purely subjective mental propensities is incorrect. But on the other hand, the objective validity of the categories does not lead us to a pure realm of intelligible realities beyond the world of sensible phenomena. The categories are valid only in so far as they lay down the conditions which must obtain if it is to be possible for us to experience the world as we do.

This outline necessarily fails to do justice to the vast array of complex arguments that make up the *Critique*.[41] It must be said however, that many of those who have delved deeper into these arguments have found that the deeper they go the more difficult and elusive Kant's position becomes. Though Kant's style is positively pellucid when contrasted with that of the German idealists (such as Fichte and Hegel) who followed him, the writing is often dense and ponderous and is couched in highly abstract language, with little in the way of specific examples to help the reader through the mass of technical jargon. This is particularly true of the crucial arguments in the 'transcendental deduction' where Kant often leaves it frustratingly unclear exactly in what sense the categories are supposed to possess their objective validity. But for all that, *The Critique of Pure Reason* remains the most important philosophical work of modern times, and it seems certain that any further progress in the perennial debate between rationalists and empiricists will have to take the Kantian analysis of human knowledge as its starting point.

NOTES

1. Letter to Mersenne 16 June 1641 in Kenny (tr.), *Descartes' Philosophical Letters* [34] p.104.
2. *Essay Concerning Human Understanding* (1690) [67] Bk. I, Ch.1, section 2.
3. *Ibid.*, I, ii, 1.
4. *Ibid.*, I, ii, 18.
5. *Ibid.*, I, ii, 4.
6. See above, Ch. 2, pp. 24–6.
7. *Essay*, I, ii, 5.
8. *Ibid.*, II, i, 1.
9. *Ibid.*
10. *Enquiry concerning Human Understanding* (1748) [73] Section II.
11. *Essay*, II, i, 6.
12. Letter to 'Hyperaspistes' August 1641 in Kenny [34] p.111.
13. *Nouveaux Essais sur l'entendement humain (New Essays on Human Understanding)*, (first published posthumously in 1765) tr. in Parkinson [55] p.150.
14. *Ibid.*, p.151.
15. *Ibid.*, p.153.
16. *New Essays*, Bk. II, Ch.1, section 2; Cf. above p.27–8.
17. *Essay*, II, i, 25.
18. See below, Ch.5, section D.
19. *A Treatise of Human Nature*, (1739–40) [72], Bk. I, Part 1, section 1.
20. *Enquiry concerning Human Understanding* [73] Section IV, part i.
21. *Ibid.*

22. *Ibid.*, Section XII, part iii.
23. *Ibid.*, Section IV, part i.
24. *Ibid.*, Section VII, part ii.
25. This imaginary example, now standardly used as an objection to the Humean account of causation, seems to have been originally employed in rather a different context by the Belgian philosopher Arnold Geulinex (1624–69). For the point about patterns of explanation cf. G. J. Warnock, 'Hume on Causation' in Pears [77].
26. *First Enquiry*, Section VII, part ii [73].
27. Cf. Mackie, *The Cement of the Universe* [79].
28. *Prolegomena to Every Future Metaphysics* (1783) tr. Lucas [83] p.9.
29. *Kritik der Reinen Vernunft* (1781); 2nd ed. 1787, B. 3, 4, [82].
30. *Ibid.*, B 232.
31. *Ibid.*, A 493, B 52.
32. *Ibid.*, A 5, B 8.
33. See above p.75–6.
34. *Kritik*, A 51, B 75.
35. *Ibid.*, A 271, B 327.
36. *Ibid.*, A 93, B 126.
37. *Treatise* [72] I, xiv.
38. *Kritik*, B 5.
39. *Ibid.*, A 89, B 122.
40. *Ibid.*, A 193, B 238.
41. For detailed analysis of the arguments of *The Critique of Pure Reason* see Scruton [84], Walker [85], Bennett [86].

V

RATIONALISM IN
THE TWENTIETH CENTURY

A. THE LEGACY OF HEGEL

TWENTIETH-CENTURY VIEWS OF HEGEL

A remarkable fact about the study of philosophy in the present century is the way in which, until quite recently, the writings of Hegel (1770–1831) were largely ignored by philosophers in the English-speaking tradition. For a time it became standard practice for university courses in the history of philosophy to reach Hume and Kant and then to jump over a hundred years, moving on to the 'analytic movement' of Bertrand Russell and G. E. Moore. Where the nineteenth century was studied, the focus tended to be on writers such as Jeremy Bentham and J. S. Mill who had vigorously kept alive the empiricist tradition (acting, as it were, as a link between Hume and Russell). 'Hegelian idealism', if mentioned at all, was cited as an example of how philosophy had gone astray; it was a paradigm case of rationalist 'web-spinning' run riot, a misguided attempt to bypass the rigorous and precise methods of experimental science and arrive at judgements about 'ultimate reality' by pure speculative reason.

A reaction against this view has now set in, and in the last two decades many philosophers have begun to appreciate that, despite his high-flown and bombastic style, Hegel has original and illuminating insights to offer about the nature of human knowledge. But the old conception dies hard: as recently as 1982 we find a commentator condemning Hegel as 'pre-empting the function of the scientist and attempting to settle *a priori* what are matters for practical investigation'.[1] So it will be useful to begin by looking at how this hostile view of Hegel arose.

THE TRADITIONAL CARICATURE: HEGEL THE 'PERFUMED DREAMER'

The long-standing tendency to dismiss Hegel (in many cases without bothering to read him) is due in large part to the assessment of Bertrand Russell. Russell, though he toyed with Hegelian ideas in his youth, soon came to consider that Hegel's views were insubstantial and inflated nonsense.

> Hegelians had all kinds of arguments to prove this or that was not 'real'. Number, space, time, matter, were all professedly convicted of being self-contradictory. Nothing was real, so we were assured, except the Absolute, which could think only of itself since there was nothing else for it to think of and which thought eternally the sort of things that idealist philosophers thought in their books.[2]

The theory caricatured and dismissed here is Hegel's so-called 'absolute idealism'. All actual events in the world can be seen, on Hegel's view, as stages towards full self-conscious rationality, the absolute 'Mind' or 'self-positing spirit' which Hegel calls *Geist*. The term 'idealism', which has a number of different meanings in philosophy, requires some explanation in the present context. Hegelians saw themselves as developing and refining the Kantian theory of knowledge. Kant, as we have seen, stressed the active role of the understanding in experiencing the world: the arguments which Kant labelled the 'transcendental deduction' tried to establish that certain fundamental concepts or 'categories' of the understanding are presupposed by the mind in its experience of the phenomenal world. But although Kant described this philosophical position as 'transcendental *idealism*' he stopped short of the claim that only the mental is real. Kant's view is that, though there may be a mind-independent world of 'things in themselves', human beings can never attain any meaningful knowledge of it; for all knowledge must necessarily relate to what is given in experience and interpreted by the mind in a certain way. The Hegelians went further than this, however, and wholly rejected the notion of 'things in themselves' as unintelligible. Only the ideal is real; all that exists must be mental.

The doctrines of 'Hegelian idealism' gradually gained an extraordinary popularity in the English-speaking world through the work of such writers as T. H. Green (1836–82) and F. H. Bradley (1846–1924) (who both held positions at Oxford), and the Cambridge philosopher John McTaggart (1866–1925). Indeed, at the turn of the century idealism of a Hegelian or quasi-Hegelian variety was the dominant philosophy in England and (to a lesser extent) America.[3] When Russell attacks Hegelian metaphysics, it is the doctrine of these English-speaking Hegelians which he seems to have principally in mind. 'Russell's Hegel', as one critic has observed, 'is vaguely recognisable as McTaggart seen through a glass darkly'.[4] McTaggart in fact proposed an extreme version of idealism which in all reality is regarded as essentially spiritual: matter, space and time are relegated to the world of mere subjective appearance. To philosophers of the analytical and mathematical school founded by Russell and Frege, such doctrines seemed pretentious and ultimately valueless; it seemed to them that this kind of philosophizing could only serve to obscure the truth in a mass of 'perfumed dreams', as one of Russell's contemporaries put it.[5]

HEGEL'S NOTION OF *GEIST*

So much for the caricature. But we must now look at Hegel's actual doctrines and see whether they really amount to the unbridled self-indulgence of a 'rationalist metaphysician' run amok. First of all, it must be conceded that if Hegel's central ontological claim about cosmic spirit or *Geist* is taken literally, then it seems to be one which there is little reason to accept. Hegel's most sympathetic and energetic present day interpreter, Professor Charles Taylor, readily admits that the doctrine is today 'quite dead. No one actually believes [Hegel's] central ontological thesis that the universe is posited by a spirit whose essence is rational necessity'.[6] Today both theists who believe in a transcendental creator, and the varieties of materialist who dispense with God altogether, unite in rejecting Hegel's self-positing *Geist* as a false (some would even say unintelligible) notion. It is, however, possible to interpret Hegel's theory of *Geist* in a more sympathetic way. For, despite the elaborate and sometimes almost mystical-sounding claims which Hegel makes for his absolute self-positing spirit, the perspective of Hegel's philosophy is not that of timeless *a priori* truths or eternal verities; Hegel is concerned above all to uncover and explain the dynamic processes of the actual historical world. Seen in this perspective, *Geist* becomes not so much a mysterious spiritual 'Absolute' in which all things partake, as an ultimate stage of development towards which history moves. *Geist*, as Hegel insists, is exemplified in the three forms of Art, Religion and Philosophy. It is not an Aristotelian prime-mover or a Cartesian eternal perfect being. Rather it emerges out of the progressive struggle of humanity to realize itself and understand the world. As J. N. Findlay has put it:

> That *Geist* is the truth of everything does not mean that *Geist* engineered the world or was causally responsible for it: *Geist* makes its appearance at a comparatively late stage in the world's history, and its supreme stage, philosophy, is even said to arrive in the world when the shades of night are falling . . . [*Geist* represents] a peculiar view of the facts of experience . . . not something which underlies the universe or is causally responsible for it.[7]

If this interpretation is correct, then the ontological core of Hegelian 'rationalism' begins to look less suspect; so far from being a piece of *a priori* metaphysics, it can be exhibited as an attempt to interpret the actual historical facts of human experience.

HEGEL'S DIALECTIC

Whatever the correct interpretation of Hegel's doctrine of *Geist* may be, it is his theory of dialectic that has provided the main impetus for the current revival of interest in Hegelian philosophy. This theory is prominent in Hegel's most famous work the *Phenomenology of Spirit (Phänomenologie des Geistes*, 1807), and also in the *Encyclopaedia (Encyclopädie der philosophischen Wissenschaften im Grundrisse*, 1817; substantially revised editions 1827, 1830). The term 'dialectic' derives ultimately from the Greek verb *dialegein*, 'to converse', and its use in philosophy first appears in Plato. In the Socratic dialogues, progress is typically made by a dynamic process of argument and counter-argument: a position is put forward, counter-examples and objections are offered, and the original position is then modified to take account of these objections. The process then repeats itself, and further adjustments are made. More technically, the term 'dialectic' is used in Plato's *Republic* to describe the highest form of philosophical reasoning, whereby the mind, using the process of argument and counter-argument, gradually ascends upwards to first principles.[8] In Hegel this Platonic notion is developed and refined in a rather special way, and the structure of philosophical reasoning emerges as essentially *triadic*: each triad (though Hegel himself did not actually use the terms in this way) consists of thesis, antithesis and synthesis. In the *thesis*, an initial position is put forward, but analysis shows that it leads to paradoxes and contradictions. These difficulties lead to the generation of the *antithesis* – the opposite of the original thesis. But the antithesis in turn proves inadequate, and the contradictions and inadequacies of both thesis and antithesis are resolved in a new position – the *synthesis*. The synthesis is what Hegel calls the *Aufhebung* of both thesis and antithesis. The term *Aufhebung* is generally translated 'sublation', but this mysterious term explains nothing; in fact Hegel's notion is a relatively straightforward one. The ordinary German verb '*aufheben*' has a dual meaning: in one sense it means 'to lift' or 'raise up'; in another sense it signifies to 'cancel out', 'nullify' or 'destroy'. Thus a Hegelian synthesis annuls or cancels out what is irrational and mistaken in both thesis and antithesis, but it also 'raises up' and preserves what is rational and true in each, and incorporates these elements into a higher truth. (The dual sense of *'aufheben'* is not, incidentally, a peculiarity of German: the Latin verb *'tollere'* can similarly mean both to lift up and to destroy. But English has no single corresponding verb, and perhaps the nearest we can get to the idea involved is by means of a pun: the synthesis 'raises' and 'razes' elements of both thesis and antithesis.)

Hegel's triadic structure does not stop with the synthesis, but repeats itself and ascends upwards. Once we have arrived at the synthesis, we can then treat it as a new thesis, which analysis can show to contain further contradictions and difficulties. The mind is thus led to posit a new antithesis, and this in turn will generate a new synthesis, and so on, until we eventually arrive at a final perspective or *Ansicht* which reveals the ultimate truth.

SENSIBLE CERTAINTY, PERCEPTION AND SELF-CONSCIOUSNESS

An example, taken from the *Phenomenology*, may serve to illustrate the dialectical movement of Hegel's thought. Initially human beings can be regarded as approaching the world by passively taking in the data revealed by the five senses. This ordinary awareness of things is called by Hegel 'sensible certainty' or 'natural awareness' (*naturliches Bewusstsein*). The way Hegel characterizes sensible certainty makes it in some ways reminiscent of the empiricist notion, developed by Locke and Hume, of the mind as a passive receptor of sensory ideas or 'impressions'.[9] But how can such awareness serve as the basis for human knowledge? According to Hegel, it cannot possibly do so, for if the mind confined itself to isolated particular impressions, it would be incapable of making any coherent judgements at all. Any attempt to make a judgement must involve *describing* our experience, and any description must necessarily go beyond the particular 'given' and make use of general or universal terms. Without universal concepts like 'red', 'round', 'large', etc., no conscious knowledge is possible. Thus the initial idea of 'sensible certainty' is shown to be a self-defeating or contradictory notion; its supposed object, an unmediated sensory impression, reduces to something 'untrue, irrational, simply gestured at' (*das Unwahre, Unvernunftige, bloss Gemeinte*).[10]

We are thus led beyond the thesis to the antithesis: from mere sensible awareness, we progress to apprehension of things as objects qualified by universal properties. This apprehension of things as possessing general properties is called by Hegel 'perception' (*Wahrnemung*). Yet this notion of perception, Hegel argues, can in turn be shown to be inadequate and contradictory. For to perceive a thing as a particular object is to conceive of it as a singular unity (*ausschliessendes Eins*); yet to describe something in terms of a group of properties is automatically to move into a different dimension – the dimension of generality and diversity. The 'contradiction' that Hegel attempts to uncover here is not at first sight an easy one to grasp: the fact that a single object (e.g. a cup) is perceived as having general properties (e.g. shape) does not seem intrinsically paradoxical or problematic. But perhaps an example (not Hegel's) may help us to glimpse something of what Hegel is getting at. If we are to ascribe the property of, for example, fragility to a cup, we are automatically moving beyond the characterization of the cup in terms of how it is at the time we perceive it; we are going beyond its directly observable properties and conceiving of it as a thing with permanent causal dispositions or powers. Our conception of the cup involves an understanding of a group of causal properties and relations; and this analysis takes us to the concept of an object as a thing possessing force or power (*Kraft*).[11]

So far, then, we have moved from an analysis of the inadequacy of sensible awareness of particulars, to the antithesis – the perception of a thing with general properties. But this kind of apprehension of things has in turn been shown to be limited and inadequate. The final step in the dialectic moves up to the synthesis – that higher species of awareness which Hegel terms 'self-consciousness' (*Selbstbewusstsein*). In order to understand objects as having causal powers we cannot simply 'perceive' them; we must *interact* with them as purposive self-conscious agents. Thus a true grasp of the world is available only to self-conscious subjects who are aware of themselves and their own active causal participation in the world around them. Our knowledge of the world presupposes our *engagement* with it as self-conscious beings.

The above summary is a (necessarily very compressed) sketch of only one of the areas where the swing of Hegel's dialectic operates, but it is perhaps enough to give some indication of the subtlety and power of his approach. There is, however, one respect at least in which our account so far may be misleading. For it may lead the reader to suppose that Hegelian dialectic is a purely abstract tool of philosophical analysis (indeed commentators often misleadingly talk of Hegel's dialectical '*method*' as if it were a philosophical implement like Descartes' method of doubt). But for Hegel, dialectic is not a mere theoretical device; it is a dynamic description of the way history actually unfolds itself as humanity gradually ascends to full self-consciousness. Thus in a famous passage in the *Phenomenology* the dialectical swing is applied to the master-slave relationship, which Hegel uses to describe the progressive liberation of the human spirit from external domination until it eventually attains full self-realization and autonomy. Or again, in the *Naturrecht und Staatswissenschaft im Grundrisse*, 1821 (generally known as *The Philosophy of Right*) Hegel presents a dialectical triad according to which obedience to an abstract moral law is the thesis, individual ethical subjectivism is the antithesis, and a rational system of social ethics (still to be fully realized) is the ultimate synthesis.

HEGEL AND RATIONALISM

Hegel's dialectical account of the emergence of self-consciousness in the *Phenomenology* is an important landmark in the development of rationalist thought. Although it by no means solves all the problems inherent in the rationalist enterprise, it does mark out one route which the rationalist philosopher can take in order to escape the impasse that confronted the great seventeenth-century metaphysicians. One of the central features of seventeenth-century rationalism was, as we have seen, its apriorism. Deductive reasoning, based on innately implanted 'clear and distinct ideas' was offered as the tool for freeing the philosopher from the misleading world of the senses and enabling him to describe the nature of ultimate reality. But this notion of 'pure' rational understanding gives rise to the awkward question of how the initial premises of the system can be guaranteed to be true. There is always the danger in the seventeenth-century metaphysical systems that the philosopher will be seen as a self-indulgent 'web-spinner' constructing elaborate systems out of nothing. Reason, it seems, is being asked to achieve the impossible and pull itself up by its own boot straps; yet how can reason possibly guarantee the truth of its own procedures? (For more about this see our earlier discussions of the 'Cartesian circle' in Chapter 3.)[12] To these doubts about the viability of the rationalist enterprise may be added the strictures developed by Kant: reason, it seems, can never transcend the phenomenal world of appearances because all understanding must necessarily operate with concepts that are presupposed in, and applicable to, sensory experience.[13]

The Hegelian notion of dialectical reasoning now presents the rationalist with a possible escape from these difficulties. First, the philosopher, on Hegel's view, does not reject sensory experience. The swing of the dialectical process reveals the inadequacies of empiricism's reliance on the passive apprehension of particular data; but this stage of sensory awareness is not simply cast aside in the search for some supposedly 'pure' uncontaminated species of perception. Ordinary sensible awareness is *aufgehoben*: its contradictions are removed but its valuable elements are preserved and 'lifted up' – reintegrated into a higher and more systematic kind of knowledge.

Secondly, the Hegelian conception shows how rationalism can escape from the charge of trying to pull itself up by its own boot straps. Instead of a deductive model of knowledge, where the initial premises are pulled out of the air by pure thought, and their consequences unfolded in a descending series of demonstrations, Hegel offers us a model of the dynamic *upward* struggle of the mind. Instead of moving downwards from self-guaranteeing truths implanted in the mind by God (as happens in the Cartesian conception), the philosopher starts, for Hegel, from our ordinary awareness, and endeavours to resolve its limitations and integrate it into a higher level of insight.

Though Hegel's style and method of philosophizing is highly original, he did not develop his approach out of nothing, and his system can be seen as drawing on some of the fundamental insights of the great rationalists who preceded him. From Plato, Hegel takes the notion of dialectical reasoning conceived as an upward struggle of the mind in its progressive attempts to achieve ultimate philosophical understanding. From Spinoza's 'holistic' conception of knowledge Hegel takes the notion that in order to understand particular events and objects we need ultimately to integrate them into a single systematic and all-embracing whole. And from the brilliant and subtle philosophy of Kant (to which he is most obviously and most directly indebted) Hegel takes the idea of the 'transcendental argument' – that is the idea of a philosophical argument which does not start *a priori*, from outside experience, but instead uncovers the structures of the understanding which are *presupposed* in experience.

NOTE ON LOGIC IN HEGEL

Hegel sometimes presents himself as developing a new kind of reasoning which, in contrast to traditional logic, willingly embraces contradiction and paradox in the attempt to develop new and fruitful insights. This has led some commentators to accuse Hegel of abandoning altogether such fundamental principles as the law of non-contradiction (which states that a proposition 'P' and its negation 'not P' cannot both be simultaneously true). Certainly there have been 'post Hegelians', particularly of the Marxist variety, who have believed themselves to be abandoning the law of non-contradiction, and have claimed Hegel as their authority for abandoning old-fashioned 'bourgeois' logic. But there is no reason to convict Hegel himself of having committed this blunder, whose only result would be to make philosophy incapable of making any meaningful assertions whatsoever.[14] In fact Hegel never simply embraces two incompatible propositions as simultaneously true and leaves it at that. The process of *Aufhebung* always requires that we transcend the contradiction, discarding what is false and integrating what is true into a new synthesis. Furthermore, there seems no reason why the traditional deductive methods of logic and the Hegelian system of dialectic should be regarded as incompatible. For while dialect may describe the upward struggles of the mind towards self-consciousness, there seems to be nothing to rule out the subsequent employment of a 'downward' deductive schema in order to unfold the consequences of the insights which dialectic has succeeded in achieving. As Descartes once observed (in a rather different connection), the method of discovery is one thing, the method of exposition another;[15] there is no reason to regard the two as being in conflict, since their aims are fundamentally different.

B. THE RISE AND FALL OF MODERN EMPIRICISM

RATIONALISM UNDER ATTACK

Despite the high esteem in which Hegelian ideas were held at the turn of the century, they were soon to be threatened by a new and vigorous tide upsurge of empiricist philosophy. Logical positivism, which was a particularly radical and uncompromising form of empiricism, took as its prime target those Hegelians who made pronouncements about 'ultimate reality' and the 'Absolute'. By 1936 we find A. J. Ayer scornfully dismissing Bradley's claim that 'the Absolute enters into but is itself incapable of evolution and progress' as a nonsensical 'pseudo-proposition', lacking any factual significance.[16] But the positivists did not restrict their attack to Hegelian idealism. The whole of traditional metaphysics was seen as suspect, and the very basis of the rationalist claim to achieve *a priori* knowledge of the nature of things was called into question. The positivist programme was nothing less than, in Ayer's words, to 'destroy the foundations of rationalism':

The fundamental tenet of rationalism is that thought is an independent source of knowledge, and is, moreover, a more trustworthy source of knowledge than experience; indeed some rationalists have gone so far as to say that thought is the only source of knowledge. And the ground for this view is simply that the only necessary truths about the world which are known to us are known through thought and not through experience. So that if we can show that either the truths in question are not necessary, or that they are not 'truths about the world' we shall be taking away the support on which rationalism rests.[17]

The strategy here outlined is one of cutting the ground from under the rationalist's feet by showing that his attempt to discover 'necessary truths' about the world is a radically misguided one. But before looking at the details of this positivist critique of rationalism, a brief word should be said of the philosophical developments that preceded it.

RUSSELL AND WITTGENSTEIN

Though neither Russell nor Wittgenstein should be classified as logical positivists, the doctrines which they articulated in the early part of this century did to some extent
pave the way for the rise of positivism. In his article 'Logic
and Mysticism' (1914), Bertrand Russell (1872–1970) put
forward an uncompromising defence of the Humean position that our knowledge of the world must be based on
sensory experience. 'Every proposition which we can
understand', Russell insists, 'must be composed wholly of
constituents with which we are acquainted'. The 'constituents' are for Russell the items which are given in sensory
experience – the 'data of the outer senses with which we are
acquainted in sensation'. Such 'sense-data', to use Russell's
preferred label (which has since become a standard term in
philosophy), typically include 'such things as colours,
smells, hardnesses, roughnesses and so on'.[18]

Sense-data are, for Russell, the fundamental building-
blocks out of which our knowledge of the world is constructed. It is of course true that many of the entities with which
science deals are not directly given in experience; points,
instants, atoms (not to mention the particles of modern
quantum theory) are not things with which we can claim to
be directly acquainted. Indeed, even the notion of an
ordinary physical object such as a chair or table, seems to
take us beyond the realm of immediate sensory data. But
Russell argues (in *Our Knowledge of the External World*, 1914)
that all these supposedly 'inferred entities' can in fact be
regarded as what he calls *logical constructions* of sense-data.[19]
Physical objects are to be interpreted as structures composed of elements which are actually experienced; or, to put
it another way, propositions about physical objects are to be
analysed into collections of propositions about sense-data.
The concept of scientific knowledge which this theory
entails is strongly empiricist. Any description of the external world, indeed the entire structure of physics, is to be
analysed as an elaborate set of constructions out of the data

presented in experience: 'The verification of physics is only possible if physical objects can be exhibited as functions of sense-data. We have to solve the equations ... so as to make them give physical objects in terms of sense-data.'[20]

As this quotation suggests, the impetus behind Russell's empiricism is primarily an epistemological one: it stems from his concern about how human knowledge is possible and how our claims to knowledge can be verified. By contrast, the doctrines of Ludwig Wittgenstein (1899–1951) in the famous *Tractatus Logico-Philosophicus* (1921) arise out of more abstract problems regarding the structure of propositions and their meaning. Wittgenstein divides propositions into two kinds, complex and simple, and, using a technique known as the 'truth-table' (which has now become standard) he shows that the truth value (truth or falsity) of a compound proposition depends on (or is a 'function' of) the truth value of the elementary propositions of which it is composed ('The proposition is a truth function of elementary propositions').[21] But what of an elementary proposition? Here Wittgenstein introduces his *picture theory* of meaning. The world is composed of 'states of affairs' (*Sachverhalten*), and the proposition (*Sach*) gets its meaning by being a kind of picture (*Bild*) of a state of affairs. 'At first sight', Wittgenstein admits, 'a proposition – one set out on the printed page for example – does not seem to be a picture of the reality with which it is concerned. But no more does musical notation at first sight seem to be a picture of music, or our phonetic notation (the alphabet) to be a picture of our speech. Yet these sign languages prove to be pictures, in even the most ordinary sense, of what they represent.'[22]

This general theory of meaning does not, as it stands, take sides in the dispute between rationalists and empiricists; indeed Wittgenstein says remarkably little about the exact nature of his states of affairs or the way in which they are to be apprehended. But where Wittgenstein's theory can be seen as influencing later empiricists is in its austere and restricted conception of the limits of philosophy. Wittgenstein's picture theory allows no place for, for example, ethical or aesthetic judgements: these cannot be genuine propositions since they are not pictures of facts in the world. If there are any 'values' asserts Wittgenstein, they must lie outside the world – outside what is the case;[23] and hence they are beyond the limits of the sayable. Even logic can assert nothing significant beyond empty tautologies, which 'say nothing', their truth being guaranteed simply by their internal structure.[24] Indeed, the whole of philosophy now becomes strictly unsayable:

> The correct method in philosophy would simply be this: to say nothing except what can be said, i.e. the propositions of natural science – i.e. something which has nothing to do with philosophy – and then, whenever someone wanted to say something metaphysical, to show him that he had failed to give a meaning to certain signs in his propositions.[25]

There is no reference here to knowledge, verification or sense-data. But Wittgenstein does hold up the scientific statement as a paradigm of meaningfulness; and secondly, he dismisses 'metaphysical' claims which fail to measure up to this paradigm as meaningless. Both these doctrines, as we shall see, were to figure centrally in the work of the logical positivists. Wittgenstein does not give any examples of the 'metaphysical' pronouncements which would fail, on his theory, to be meaningful. But it seems clear that many of the claims of the great seventeenth-century rationalists would have to be regarded, on Wittgenstein's view, as going beyond the limits of the sayable. Indeed, any philosophical system that goes beyond strictly scientific descriptions of what 'is the case' would seem to violate the stern warning with which Wittgenstein closes the *Tractatus:* '*Wovon man nicht sprechen kann, daruber muss man schweigen*' ('What cannot be spoken of must be passed over in silence').

LOGICAL POSITIVISM AND THE ELIMINATION OF METAPHYSICS

The term 'logical positivism' has become the standard label to refer to the doctrines originally put forward by the so-called 'Vienna Circle' of philosophers, scientists and mathematicians which flourished in the 1920s and '30s. The group's leading members included Moritz Schlick, Rudolph Carnap and Otto Neurath; and the movement's leading exponent in the English-speaking world was A. J. Ayer, who published his celebrated *Language, Truth and Logic* after visiting Vienna in 1933 as a young graduate student. As already noted, the positivist programme aimed to undermine the foundations of rationalism; indeed, all 'metaphysical' pronouncements in philosophy were to be eliminated: 'no statement which refers to a "reality" transcending the limits of all possible sense-experience can possibly have any literal significance; from which it follows that the labours of those who have striven to describe such a reality have all been devoted to the production of nonsense.' The tool for the elimination of metaphysics was the famous principle of verification: 'a sentence is factually significant to a given person if, and only if, he knows how to verify the proposition which it purports to express.'[26]

The logical positivist thus presented rationalism with a formidable challenge: could such claims as those made by Spinoza about substance, or by Leibniz about monads, or by Hegel about the Absolute, be verified? 'Verification', it should be noted, was initially construed by the positivists in a very strict way: a proposition was held to be verifiable only if there were *observation statements* that could directly establish its truth or falsity. This crucial test – the ability to be tested directly against observation statements – was one which traditional rationalist theories seemed conspicuously unable to meet. Indeed, so far from being able to back up their claims by observational results, some rationalists had appeared to display a positive disdain for empirical observation and insist that philosophical inquiry could proceed independently of the senses.[27]

It seems at first that the rationalist has a powerful argument to support his claim that there are truths of reason which can be established independently of experience. Surely logical and mathematical statements, at least, are perfectly meaningful; yet they do not require to be verified experimentally or observationally. And if, despite their *a priori* character, logical and mathematical truths count as genuine contributions to human knowledge, how can the positivist be justified in dismissing the other claims of the rationalists, simply because they are not arrived at via observation?

The positivist reply here was to allow that the propositions of logic and mathematics are independent of experience, but to argue that such propositions are true by definition – that is, true simply and solely in virtue of the meanings of the symbols involved. Thus 'either hamburgers are nutritious or they are not nutritious' is indeed true, necessarily true, independent of experience; but its truth depends solely on the way in which the operators 'either-or' and 'not' are defined. (Similarly, '2 + 2 = 4' depends for its truth simply on the meanings of the symbols involved.) It follows from this account that the propositions of logic and mathematics fail to make any factual assertion about the world. The proposition quoted above does not give us any information at all about hamburgers; it is a tautology, compatible with any possible state of affairs, and will remain true whatever terms you substitute for 'hamburger' and 'nutritious'. Thus, despite their being undeniably and necessarily true, tautologies, as Wittgenstein expressed it in his oracular fashion, 'say nothing'.[28]

Thus, so far from providing an escape route for the rationalist, the propositions of logic and mathematics seem merely to enable the positivist to tighten the net. For any meaningful proposition will now fall into one of two categories: either (1) it will be true by definition – a mere tautology – in which case it will buy its certainty and necessity at the cost of failing to make any substantive claim about the world; or else (2) it will purport to make a genuine claim about the world, but in that case observation will always be required to establish whether it happens to be true or false. And if a proposition is neither tautologous nor verifiable by observation, then the positivist will insist that it must be discarded as meaningless.

> There can be no a priori knowledge of reality. For . . . the truths of pure reason, the propositions which we know to be valid independently of all experience, are so only in virtue of their lack of factual content . . . [By contrast] empirical propositions are one and all hypotheses which may be confirmed or discredited in actual sense experience.[29]

It is important to realize the sweeping nature of the positivist attack on traditional philosophy. All philosophical claims which purported to be more than mere tautologies had to pass the test of empirical verifiability if they were to be allowed to be meaningful. And so those who wished to pursue the great rationalist inquiries into being, substance, necessity, God, causation and freedom were all faced with the challenge of specifying how, if at all, the questions they raised could be settled with reference to actual observation. Positivists were in no doubt that the effect of their challenge would be the gradual withering away of traditional rationalist philosophy. As Moritz Schlick expressed it: 'Philosophical writers will continue to discuss the old pseudo-questions. But in the end they will no longer be listened to: they will come to resemble actors who continue to play for some time before noticing that the audience has slowly departed.'[30]

THE DEMISE OF POSITIVISM

For a time the logical positivist programme for the elimination of metaphysics seemed unstoppable; its eventual collapse was not due to any rationalist counter-attack but to internal tensions and difficulties. One much discussed issue was the status of the verification principle itself. Was the principle itself verifiable, and if so how? If the principle was supposed to be an empirical hypothesis about how the term 'meaningful' was normally employed, then it seemed to be clearly false; for ordinary usage patently does not restrict the term 'meaningful' to statements that can be verified by observation. The solution eventually adopted by most positivists was that the principle was not a factual claim at all, but some sort of recommendation;[31] but this move concedes that there may be kinds of discourse that are useful and important even though their role is not that of stating empirical facts. Today, many philosophers would argue that any system of thought must have at its centre certain fundamental principles or assumptions that are not directly checkable against experience; every system must have its own 'metaphysics'. Thus, despite their professed elimination of all metaphysical claims, it seems that the positivists did in fact rely on one central metaphysical doctrine – the principle of verifiability itself.

The major difficulty that preoccupied the positivists themselves, however, concerned the status of the theoretical statements of natural science. Natural science was held up by the positivists as the paradigm of meaningful discourse; indeed Ayer had gone so far as to claim (in the closing paragraphs of *Language, Truth and Logic*) that 'philosophy is virtually empty without science; . . . philosophy must develop into the logic of science'. But how are the statements of science to be verified? Singular observational reports ('this liquid in this tube is turning red') seem verifiable enough (though conclusive verification even of this type of statement presents problems which will be omitted here); but what about 'all water at a given atmospheric pressure boils at 100 degrees Celsius'? Since this statement has the form of an unrestricted universal generalization, it follows that no finite number of observations can conclusively establish its truth. An additional and perhaps even more worrying problem is that when we reach the higher levels of science – the levels of theoretical explanation – we tend to encounter structures and entities that are not observable in any straightforward sense. Atoms, molecules, electrons, photons and the like are highly complex theoretical constructs whose properties are often specified in terms of abstract mathematical models; here we seem to be very far removed from the world of direct 'empirical observation'. It begins to look as if empiricism is quite unable to accommodate its own darling, natural science, within the verifiability principle.

The positivists tended to respond to this difficulty by weakening their criterion of meaningfulness. Since conclusive verifiability was evidently too stringent a test to accommodate universal statements, and direct observability was evidently too stringent to allow for the entities of theoretical physics, it was proposed that a statement was meaningful if it could be confirmed or supported by sensory experience.[32] However, this weaker criterion is uncomfortably vague, and of the many attempts to come up with a more precise and vigorous formulation, none proved to be entirely satisfactory. But what is crucial for our purposes here is that a weaker standard of verifiability seems generous enough to allow as meaningful the very metaphysical statements that the positivists were so concerned to exclude. Statements about God or Freedom, or the nature of Substance, or the Absolute, may not be directly checkable against experience, but it can plausibly be claimed that at least *some* observations, somewhere along the line, will be relevant to their truth or falsity. The positivist thus seems to be faced with a fatal dilemma: either he will have to make his criterion so stringent that it will exclude the generalizations and theoretical statements of science, or else he will have to weaken his criterion sufficiently to open the door to the speculations of the metaphysician. The dilemma has remained unsolved to this day, and many former positivists have come to admit that it is insoluble.

THE AFTERMATH OF POSITIVISM

The failure of the positivists to formulate a satisfactory principle of verification led to a general consensus among philosophers that the kind of extreme and rigorous empiricism which positivists envisaged is untenable. Language, including scientific language, is not checkable against observation in terms of a straightforward one-to-one correspondence; it is not feasible to specify for each and every statement some neat and tidy observation, or set of observations, which will conclusively establish its truth or falsity. It follows that if whatever goes beyond direct observations is to be classed as 'metaphysics', then there will be a good deal of metaphysics even in the language of the natural scientist. The scientist confronts the world not by measuring each individual statement against observational results; rather, he deploys a complex and elaborate system of propositions, some of which may directly record observations, but others of which are too abstract or too general, or both, to be capable of verification.

It might be supposed that the collapse of positivism would have left the way open for a resurgence of rationalist ideas. Certainly 'metaphysics' is no longer a dirty word among contemporary philosophers; and few, if any, would rule a philosophical theory out of court in advance merely because it went beyond the limits of the strictly observable. But nevertheless a rationalist revival has conspicuously failed to materialize. There seem to be two main reasons for this. First, even after the collapse of positivism, many philosophers continued to insist that any theory which purports to impart information about reality must be capable of yielding experimental or observational consequences; the leading figure here is Karl Popper, whose highly influential principle of falsifiability requires that a scientific theory be capable of being refuted by experience, even though it cannot be verified. Secondly, and more recently, the whole viability of the rationalist enterprise has come under attack from what may be loosely called a 'relativist' movement in the philosophy of science and the theory of knowledge. These two important developments will be examined in the final section (F) of this chapter.

C. RATIONALISM AND ANALYTIC PHILOSOPHY

Much of mainstream analytic philosophy since the demise of positivism has been concerned with examining the nature of meaning and truth, and it is beyond the scope of this volume to trace the recent rich and complex developments in this area. But our survey of rationalism in the twentieth century would not be complete without a brief look at the way in which two American philosophers, W. V. O. Quine (born 1908) and Saul Kripke (born 1941) have redrawn some of the boundaries within which the debate between rationalists and empiricists had hitherto been conducted.

QUINE'S ATTACK ON THE 'DOGMA' OF ANALYTICITY

We have seen how the positivist attack on rationalism relied on a fundamental distinction between two types of proposition – on the one hand the proposition which is true merely in virtue of the meanings of the symbols involved, and on the other hand the proposition which has a substantive factual component and whose truth depends on the way the world in fact is. Following the terminology first introduced by Kant [33] propositions of the former type have come to be known as *analytic*, while the latter are known as *synthetic*. The positivist thesis, expressed in terms of this distinction, is that the only propositions which we can know to be true *a priori* (independently of experience) are analytic truths – the tautologies of logic and mathematics whose truth follows from the way in which their constituent symbols are defined. And correspondingly, all synthetic propositions, propositions which purport to express some substantive, non-trivial claim about some matter of fact, must be verified *a posteriori*, by empirical observation. The positivists thus divided all meaningful propositions into two exhaustive and mutually exclusive categories:

112

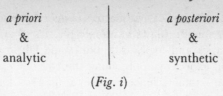

(Fig. i)

It followed from this categorization that many of the traditional claims of rationalism were ruled out of court. For many rationalists had attempted to cross the barrier in the above diagram and assert that philosophical truths could be known *a priori*, independently of experience, while at the same time being synthetic, i.e. providing substantive information about reality.

In a landmark paper entitled 'Two dogmas of empiricism' (1951) Quine mounted a radical attack on the 'dogma of analyticity' – the idea that there is a hard and fast cleavage between analytic and synthetic statements. His strategy is first to show that the notion of the analytic cannot be properly specified: all attempts to define what makes a statement analytic are open to the charge of circularity. From here he goes on to suggest that the prevailing doctrine of two *kinds* of truth, truth-in-virtue-of-meaning and truth-in-virtue-of-fact, is untenable.

> One is tempted to suppose . . . that the truth of a statement is somehow analysable into a linguistic component and a factual component. Given this supposition, it next seems reasonable that in some statements the factual component should be null; and these are the analytic statements. But for all its a priori reasonableness, a boundary between analytic and synthetic statements simply has not been drawn. That there is such a distinction to be drawn at all is an unempirical dogma of empiricists, a metaphysical article of faith.[34]

The second part of Quine's strategy is to attack 'the dogma of reductionism' – the idea that the significance of a proposition can be understood, and its truth or falsity established, in isolation. For Quine, it is not the individual statement that confronts the world, but a total system of beliefs and theories. 'The totality of our so called knowledge

113

... from the most casual matters of geography and history to the profoundest laws of atomic physics or even of pure mathematics and logic, is a man-made fabric which impinges on experience only along the edges. Or, to change the figure, total science is like a field of force whose boundary conditions are experience'.[35] Thus, in place of the neat division expressed in our diagram above, we have something more like the following:

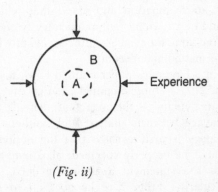

(Fig. ii)

Some of our beliefs, those lying near the periphery (in area B) are more susceptible to modification in the light of experience, and thus correspond to those traditionally characterized as 'synthetic', while those in area A, nearer the centre, are less likely to be abandoned. But this is only a matter of degree; there is no hard and fast line between two different types of truth here. And though the 'inner' truths may include many of those traditionally regarded as analytic, they do not enjoy any privileged status; they are not 'purely linguistic' truths, immune from revision.

A conflict with experience at the periphery occasions readjustments in the interior of the field ... Having re-evaluated one statement, we must re-evaluate some others, which may be statements logically connected with the first or may be the statements of logical connections themselves. But ... there is much latitude of choice as to what statements to re-evaluate in the light of any single contrary experience.[36]

Quine's arguments certainly do not constitute a defence of rationalism – indeed the tenor of most of his philosophy is firmly empiricist: 'as an empiricist, I continue to think of the conceptual scheme of science as a tool, ultimately, for predicting future experience in the light of past experience'.[37] But what his arguments do establish is that the brutal dismissal of rationalism to be found in Hume and the positivists is altogether too swift. But wielding 'Hume's fork', as the schema characterized in Fig. i has come to be known, the positivists had tried to impale the rationalists on one of two prongs: either their claims must be analytic, in which case, though knowable *a priori*, they would ultimately turn out to be empty tautologies; or else they must be synthetic, in which case the rationalists could be challenged to show how their truth could be confirmed *a posteriori*, by observation. Quine's picture, by eliminating the dogmas of analyticity and reductionism, reopens the possibility that a philosophical proposition which does not stick neatly on either of Hume's prongs could still be a genuine contribution to our knowledge; for it might be capable of being integrated, alongside the statements of logic and of science, into a total system of beliefs which confronts the world as a whole, rather than piecemeal. The upshot is a view of knowledge which is not automatically hostile to the type of holistic philosophical system envisaged by Spinoza, say, or Hegel. This is not to say that Quine defends such enterprises – far from it. But his arguments at least challenge the dogmatic empiricism which would condemn them without a hearing.

KRIPKE AND THE REVIVAL OF ESSENTIALISM

A recurring element in the rationalist enterprise is its attempt to uncover *necessary* truths about the essential nature of reality. The Platonic and Aristotelian models of knowledge both involve the idea that philosophical (and scientific) understanding is concerned with what in some sense 'must' be the case, or with what 'cannot be otherwise'.

And Descartes, Spinoza and Leibniz all, in different degrees, attempt to construct philosophical systems whose fundamental principles tell us not merely what *happens* to be true but what *must* be true.

To the empiricist, this seems fundamentally misguided. According to the powerful arguments of Hume, necessity is something which is confined to the realm of ideas or concepts. A statement like 'all triangles are three-sided' is indeed necessary, logically necessary; but this necessity derives simply from the definitions of the terms involved, and hence can produce no information about the world. By contrast, a statement which has a factual content, which purports to describe reality, must, if it is true at all, be true *contingently*. As Hume puts it: 'that the sun will not rise tomorrow is no less intelligible a proposition and implies no more contradiction, than the affirmation that it will rise.'[38] It follows, on this argument, that we must mistrust any philosopher who claims *both* that his propositions are necessary *and* that they give us information about reality. A statement can be necessary only at the cost of being ultimately uninformative; and, conversely, if a statement is informative, if it tells us what is actually the case, then it has the status of a contingent proposition – it tells us something that might have been otherwise.

A crucial premise in this anti-rationalist argument is that there is only one kind of necessity – the kind of necessity which is a function of linguistic conventions and logical rules. But those rationalists who supposed they were uncovering necessary truths about the world evidently did not believe themselves merely to be investigating the conventions of logic and language. The kind of necessity which they supposed their propositions to possess was not a mere verbal, or '*de dicto*' necessity, but a real, or '*de re*' necessity. That is, they supposed themselves to be describing not simply properties necessarily attaching to our ideas or concepts, but properties necessarily attaching to real things in the world.

Does this notion of 'real' necessity make sense? One

might be tempted to think not. Consider the proposition 'lead is malleable'. Is this a necessary truth about the world? Surely not, the Humean would argue. That the stuff we call lead is malleable is a purely contingent fact: lead might have turned out to be non-malleable, and there is no contradiction in supposing that this might have been the case. Of course we could stipulate that nothing can count as lead unless it has the property of malleability, and this will turn 'lead is malleable' into a necessary truth. But such a move buys necessity at the cost of making our proposition a tautology which is empty of factual content. Knowing the definitional truth 'lead is malleable' tells us nothing about the world – nothing about whether any given lump of bluish grey metal has the property of malleability. The truth of this latter question still remains unknown until we have conducted the requisite investigations. And the requisite investigations will be concerned with what in actual fact happens to be the case: they will take us away from necessity into the world of contingent fact.

In a highly influential series of lectures published in 1972 under the title *Naming and Necessity*, Saul Kripke casts doubt on the type of argument just sketched, and attempts to show that there can be necessarily true statements which describe essential properties of things in the world. According to Kripke, science 'attempts, by investigating basic structural traits, to find the nature, and thus the essence (in the philosophical sense) of natural kinds'.[39] (By 'natural kinds' is meant the kinds of things which occur naturally in the world, e.g. animal, vegetable and chemical kinds like blood, cellulose or lead.) This notion of science as an investigation of the 'essence' of natural kinds is an ancient one, which goes back to Aristotle. Moreover, it is a notion which – traditionally at any rate – had been associated with a rationalist outlook; for radical empiricists like Hume refused to attach any meaning to the notion of 'essential' characteristics of things. (The world, for Hume, consists of purely contingent correlations between phenomena; it makes no sense on his view, to suppose that there are 'essential' links to be discovered.) Now Aristotle, it will be remembered, asserts that scientific truths are necessary: statements about the essences of things express truths that cannot be otherwise.[40] And Kripke categorically agrees: 'such theoretical identifications as "heat is molecular energy" are *necessary*'.[41]

Initially this seems puzzling, for surely what scientists discover when they investigate the properties of things are fresh contingent facts about the way the world is – facts which might have been otherwise. Heat might not have turned out to be molecular motion; gold might not have turned out to be an element (it might, for example, have turned out to be a compound or a mixture). But this is precisely what Kripke denies. The argument here hinges on Kripke's highly controversial theory of meaning (the background to which will have to be omitted here) which suggests that the meaning of terms for natural kinds is fixed by reference to a given sample. 'Terms for natural kinds (e.g. animal, vegetable and chemical kinds) get their reference fixed in this way; the substance is defined as the kind instantiated by (almost all of) a given sample.'[42] Thus, terms like 'gold' are what Kripke calls, 'rigid designators'; that is, they uniquely name or pick out a certain substance in somewhat the same way in which a proper name like 'Aristotle' uniquely picks out a certain individual. Gold, then, rigidly designates a particular real substance with certain properties; it picks out that substance not just in our actual world, but, as Kripke puts it 'in all possible worlds'. The invoking of 'possible worlds' has puzzled some readers, who have regarded it as a bizarre piece of metaphysics. But the idea of possible worlds which differ from our own actual world is not a new one (it appears in the philosophy of Leibniz), and its cash value in Kripke's argument is relatively straightforward. Once the meaning of the term 'gold' is fixed by its being applied to a certain sample, then the term keeps its reference in all imaginable situations (including 'counterfactual' scenarios – those which might have turned out to be the case, but did not as a matter of fact occur). Given Kripke's theory of meaning it is no longer open to us to say that gold might as a matter of fact have turned out to be a compound rather than an element. Gold, this substance which is rigidly designated by the term 'gold', must necessarily be an element. As Kripke puts it:

There can be no case in which possibly gold might not have been an element. Given that gold *is* this element, any other substance, even though it looks like gold, would not be gold. It would be some other substance which was a counterfeit for gold. In any counterfactual situation where the same geographical areas were filled with such a substance, they would not have been filled with gold. They would have been filled with something else.[43]

The upshot is that statements about the structural properties of natural kinds turn out, on Kripke's analysis, to be not contingent, but necessary truths.

The validity of Kripke's neo-essentialist philosophy hinges on whether his theory of meaning is correct, and there is no space to discuss the complex arguments involved here, which remain the subject of heated debate among philosophers.[44] But if they were to gain general acceptance, Kripke's ideas would represent a striking revival of one strand in rationalism, namely its conception of science as an attempt to uncover necessary truths about reality. What the Kripkean position does, if sound, is to remove one standard objection to rationalism, by undermining the Humean thesis that there can be no necessary truths which provide information about the real world. It should be stressed however that Kripke's arguments must not, any more than those of Quine, be construed as providing a general vindication of rationalism. Although he can be regarded as reviving an Aristotelian or 'essentialist' idea of scientific knowledge, Kripke does not in any way support the idea found in some rationalists that such knowledge of reality can be arrived at *a priori*, independently of experience. There is no suggestion in Kripke of the type of apriorism which we find, say, in Plato; nor does Kripke's analysis support the Kantian notion of 'synthetic *a priori*' knowledge.

On the contrary, Kripke frequently stresses that necessary truths about the essences of natural kinds must be discovered *a posteriori*, by scientific investigation. 'The type of property identity used in sciences seems to be associated with *necessity*, not with a prioricity or analyticity. For example, the coextensiveness of the predicates "hotter" and "having higher mean molecular kinetic energy" is *necessary* but not *a priori*.'[45] Kripke thus offers no hope to the extreme type of rationalism that aims to transcend the limits of sensory experience altogether in its quest for 'essential reality'.

D. KNOWLEDGE AND LANGUAGE: THE REVIVAL OF INNATISM

In a collection of philosophical essays published in 1969 under the title *Language and Philosophy*, the editor speaks of a 'recent counter-revolution in philosophy which claims that the empiricist tradition in knowledge from Locke down is false and the rationalistic tradition of Leibniz is sound.'[46] We have already looked at the origins of the debate referred to here, contrasting Locke's view of the mind as a blank sheet, or *tabula rasa*, waiting to be written on by experience, with the Leibnizian position that the mind is already structured (like a block of marble veined in a certain pattern) in a manner which predisposes it to interpret experience in a certain way.[47] The central figure in the modern revival of this dispute is the American philosopher and linguistic scientist Noam Chomsky (born 1928).

CHOMSKY'S THEORY OF LANGUAGE ACQUISITION

The fundamental problem which Chomsky addresses is that of language acquisition. How do human infants, who come into the world clearly unproficient in English, French, Japanese or whatever, manage to acquire, in such a relatively short time, such remarkable linguistic proficiency? How do they manage, by the time they are around three years old, to understand and produce such a wide variety of grammatical sentences in English, French, Japanese or whatever?

Chomsky's starting point is an attack on the ruling empiricist model of language acquisition, championed, amongst others, by the behaviourist B. F. Skinner (born 1904).[48] The empiricists had proposed a kind of stimulus-response theory of language acquisition: by means of the constant repetition of a word whenever the appropriate sensory stimulus was presented, coupled with appropriate techniques of 're-enforcement', parents and teachers were able to set up a 'habit-structure' in the child, whereby it associated the word with the relevant stimulus, and thus in time became disposed to respond in an appropriate manner whenever presented with the stimulus in question. A key feature of this empiricist model is its stress on sensory data; the acquisition of language is seen as being ultimately a function of the presentation of the appropriate sensory stimuli at appropriate times and in appropriate combinations, via the five senses.

In criticizing this approach, Chomsky stresses the re-markable *meagreness* of the data which are presented to the young language learner, in comparison with the extent of the linguistic competence which he acquires in a very short time:

> The competence of an adult, or even a young child, is such that we must attribute to him a knowledge of language that extends far beyond anything that he has learned. Compared with the number of sentences that a child can produce or interpret with ease, the number of seconds in a lifetime is ridiculously small. Hence the data available as input is only a minute sample of the linguistic material that has been thoroughly mastered, as indicated by actual performance.[49]

Closely connected with the point about the gap between data and knowledge is the phenomenon of what Chomsky calls *creativity* in language use. It is a remarkable fact that once we have achieved a modest competence in, say English, we can every day both interpret, and ourselves produce, new sentences – sentences that we have never heard before. This, for Chomsky, marks a fundamental distinction between genuine language, and the sounds emitted by animals (e.g. barking of dogs, or birdsong): such sounds are inevitably tied to the occurrence of a given type of stimulus, whereas human language is 'stimulus free'; the creative and innovative language user is not simply responding to a given environmental stimulus, or to some internal state (like the contraction of his stomach). 'By the creative aspect of language use', says Chomsky, 'I mean the ability to produce and interpret new sentences in independence of "stimulus-control" – i.e. external stimuli or independently identifiable internal states. The normal use of language is "creative" in this sense, as was widely noted in traditional rational linguistic theory. The sentences used in everyday discourse are not "familiar sentences" or "generalizations of familiar sentences" in terms of any known process of generalization.'[50]

In order to explain these facts about human language and its acquisition, Chomsky proposes the hypothesis that all humans are born with an innate knowledge of the principles of what he calls 'universal grammar'. This innate universal grammar is not concerned with the superficial grammatical features of language, which of course differ widely from language to language (the surface grammar of English is quite different from that of Japanese, for example). Despite the surface differences, there is, Chomsky argues, a quite specific 'deep structure' common to all human languages (this deep structure is a 'system of abstract categories and phrases' such as 'logical subject', 'noun phrase', 'verb phrase', etc.[51]). Because the child possesses an innate knowledge of the principles of universal grammar it is able to learn any human language; indeed it is a familiar fact that, e.g. an Anglo-Saxon child born in England and then moved to Japan will be able to master Japanese just as easily as it would have mastered English.

What happens, according to Chomsky, is that the child, when confronted with the data of a particular language, 'maps' the surface features onto the deep grammar of which it has innate knowledge, and thus succeeds in constructing a coherent grammatical model enabling it to interpret and produce new sentences of the language in question.

CHOMSKY'S 'RATIONALISM'

Chomsky specifically uses the word 'rationalist' to characterize his theory:

It would be historically accurate to describe [my] views regarding language structure ... as a rationalist conception of the nature of language. Furthermore [they support] what might fairly be called a rationalist conception of the acquisition of knowledge, if we take the essence of this view to be that the general character of knowledge, the categories in which it is expressed or internally represented, and the basic principles that underlie it, are determined by the nature of the mind. In our case, the schematism assigned as an innate property to the language acquisition device determines the form of knowledge ... The role of experience is only to cause the innate schematism to be activated ...[52]

Just as, for Leibniz, experiential stimuli are like the hammer-blows which merely uncover a pre-existing shape in the structure of the marble, so Chomsky argues that the data to which the language learner is subjected merely 'activate' the abstract linguistic structures that are genetically programmed in the brains of the members of our species.

The notion that sensory data *underdetermine* our knowledge, which is the central strand in Chomsky's argument, is indeed to be found in the earlier rationalist thinkers. Apart from the case of Leibniz, we have seen Plato arguing in the *Meno* that the slave-boy can come to see the truth of a geometrical proposition without any observation or experiment, but purely by consulting his (apparently) innate intuitions about geometrical properties.[53] Again, Descartes denies that the ideas of geometrical ideas came into our mind via the senses. For 'there are no such figures in our environment except ones so small that they cannot in any

way impinge on our senses . . . Hence when in our childhood, we first happened to see a triangular figure drawn on
paper, it cannot have been this figure which showed us how
we should conceive of the true triangle . . . the idea of the
true triangle was already in us'.[54]

Nevertheless, Chomsky's use of the notion of innate
knowledge is importantly different from that of Plato,
Descartes or Leibniz. For by 'innate knowledge' these
philosophers had meant either explicit awareness of certain
concepts and truths (e.g. geometrical concepts and truths),
or at least the ability to achieve such awareness, given
suitable sensory stimuli. But clearly a child does not have
awareness in this sense of the principles of universal
grammar. For the principles in question involve highly
complex abstract categories and rules of transformation
which can be formulated, if at all, only by advanced
specialists in linguistic theory. In reply to this objection
Chomsky has referred to those rationalists, notably Leibniz,
who have suggested that our 'innate knowledge' need not
involve explicit awareness, but might consist of 'inclinations, dispositions, habits or powers'.[55] But this will not do.
For although the Leibnizian conception does not require
explicit awareness of innate principles, it does require that
the child be able to recognize the principles as obvious once
the appropriate stimuli have called them forth. (Similarly,
on Plato's model, we can recognize such innate principles as
self-evident and obvious, once a skilful Socratic 'midwife'
has drawn them out of us by asking the right questions.)
Chomsky's principles however, are innate *neither* in the
sense that we are explicitly aware of them, *nor* in the sense
that we have a disposition to recognize their truth as
obvious under appropriate circumstances. And hence it is
by no means clear that Chomsky is correct in seeing his
theory as following the traditional rationalist account of the
acquisition of knowledge.

What seems to have caused the confusion here is not the
notion of innateness, but the notion of *knowledge*. Clearly –
and no sane empiricist would deny this – human beings

have the capacity to do many things which other beings – tadpoles, for example – cannot do. Hence to say that our abilities and performances are 'underdetermined' by the sensory data is, in one way, obvious common sense. No amount of sensory stimulation will enable a tadpole to talk or to learn to play chess; and hence any sensible philosopher, whether rationalist or empiricist, must allow that there are some structural differences between human beings and tadpoles which are innate, or genetically determined. But evidence of innate structural properties, or even of 'capacities and dispositions' is still very far from justifying talk of *knowledge*. We all have the innate capacity to digest food, but it would be perverse and misleading to characterize this in terms of an innate knowledge of the principles of digestion. We do not, most of us, know anything at all about the principles of digestion – we just do digest food, given the appropriate stimuli. The fact that we do so is undoubtedly a function not just of the environment but of the innate, genetically determined properties of the stomach and other organs. But few, apart from specialists in physiology, have knowledge of those principles. The parallel with language acquisition seems obvious. No doubt there are complex principles involved, but none except a few linguistic specialists have either an explicit awareness of these principles or even a disposition to recognize their truth. Language acquisition is something we just do, without any conscious reflection on the principles involved.

It seems then that the parallel which Chomsky himself draws between his theories and the traditional rationalist doctrine of innate ideas is more misleading than helpful. And there is one other respect in which it may be misleading to characterize Chomsky's views as 'rationalistic'. Most proponents of innateness were strongly committed to the idea of *a priori* knowledge – indeed the commitment to such knowledge was one powerful motive for asserting that some of our ideas are innate. Chomsky follows this tradition in one respect: the child's knowledge of the principles of universal grammar is, he claims, *a priori* rather than acquired via experience. But as far as the philosophical status of his own linguistic theories is concerned, Chomsky is certainly not an apriorist. On the contrary, he makes it clear that his theory of innate universal grammar is an empirical hypothesis to be tested against the facts of psychology (i.e. evidence about the ways in which children learn language), and physiology (i.e. evidence about the structure and wiring of our brains).

Nevertheless, it is correct to see Chomsky as belonging to that substantial group of recent thinkers who have reacted against the extreme and dogmatic empiricism that dominated philosophy and science during much of this century. Thus he rejects the 'black-box' model of psychology, which attempts to explain human behaviour purely in terms of observed correlations between inputs and outputs, in favour of an investigation of the structures and mechanisms which may explain how that behaviour is produced. And in this general sense, Chomsky can be regarded as sympathetic to the Aristotelian and Leibnizian tradition, which sees science as concerned with the essential inner structure of substances, as opposed to the Humean view which regards scientific knowledge as reducible to a series of observed correlations.

CHOMSKY AND CARTESIAN LINGUISTICS

There is one other important reason why Chomsky is often thought of as reviving the rationalist tradition, and that is his allegiance to the Cartesian view that language is a uniquely human capacity. The empiricist linguists against whom Chomsky reacted had tended to underline the similarities between human 'linguistic responses' and apparently similar kinds of responses to be found in other animals. Chomsky however insists that the genuine use of language is, as he puts it, 'species-specific' – unique to homo sapiens. His position here is remarkably similar to that of Descartes, who, three centuries earlier, had insisted on a fundamental divide between animal behaviour and human language:

126

If you teach a magpie to say good-day to its mistress, when it sees her approach, this can only be by making the utterance of the word the expression of one of its passions. For instance it will be the expression of the hope of eating, if it has always been given a titbit when it says the word. Similarly, all the things which dogs, horses and monkeys are taught to perform are only expressions of their fear, their hope or their joy ... But the use of words, so defined, is peculiar to human beings.[56]

Chomsky explicitly sides with the Cartesians in holding that 'an animal can operate on the principle of the speedo-meter – producing a ... continuous set of signals as output in response to a continuous range of stimuli'. But human language, he maintains, is entirely different:

A person who knows a language has mastered a set of rules and principles that determine an infinite discrete set of sentences each of which has a fixed form and a fixed meaning or meaning-potential. Even at the lowest level of intelligence, the characteristic use of this knowledge is free and creative in the sense just described and in that one can instantaneously interpret an inde-finitely large range of utterances with no feeling of unfamiliarity or strangeness ... If this is correct, then it is quite pointless to speculate about the 'evolution' of human language from animal communication systems.[57]

The idea, shared by Descartes and Chomsky, that our linguistic abilities indicate a special type of freedom from environmental determinants of behaviour is an important and exciting one. But the parallel between Cartesian and Chomskean linguistics should not be stretched too far. For Descartes, linguistic capacities are a function of the non-physical, unextended and indivisible soul which God has conjoined to our bodies; for Chomsky, the explanation of these capacities must be sought ultimately in the physical structure of our brains (and the fundamental gap between humans and animals here suggests that the emergence of language must have been due to a distinct evolutionary jump associated with some mutation in the brain-structure of our ancestors).

Perhaps Chomsky's most important contribution on the

philosophical front is to have drawn our attention to how special and remarkable is the ability to learn language which every normal child possesses. In insisting that such an apparently straightforward and obvious phenomenon is in need of analysis and explanation, Chomsky is making an original contribution which does not fit neatly into either the rationalist or the empiricist tradition. For classical philosophy of mind, both rationalist and empiricist had made the 'unquestioned assumption that the properties and contents of the mind are accessible to intuition'.[58] Thinkers as far apart as Descartes and Hume had subscribed to the theory of the 'perfect transparency of the mind' – the thesis that the mind is like a transparent bowl within which all mental contents or 'ideas' are readily locatable, so that we only have to focus on any given idea in order to be aware of it. For Chomsky, we have no privileged access to the contents and workings of the mind, any more than we have in the case of any other phenomenon to be studied by science. The 'data' – our linguistic performances and the linguistic intuitions we have about those performances – are given; but the organizing principles and underlying mechanisms remain to be discovered. It is Chomsky's achievement to have stimulated much detailed empirical research and philosophical reflection about the precise nature of these principles and mechanisms.[59]

E. RATIONALISM IN ETHICS

THE EIGHTEENTH-CENTURY BACKGROUND

The term 'rationalism' is nowadays more often associated with theoretical issues in philosophy (such as the nature and origins of human knowledge) rather than the practical concerns of morality. But in the eighteenth century it was quite common for philosophers to lump theoretical and practical principles together, and to offer the same type of account – one which may fairly be described as rationalistic

– of both 'natural, and 'moral' knowledge. Thus Samuel Clarke (1675–1729) writes:

> It was a very wise observation of Plato ... that if you take a young man ... that never had any learning nor any experience in the world; and examine him about the *natural relations and proportions* of things or the *moral differences* of *good and evil*; you may, only by asking him questions, without teaching him anything at all directly, cause him to express in his answers just and adequate notions of *geometrical truths*, and true and exact determinations concerning *matters of right and wrong* ... This proves unavoidably ... that the differences, relations and proportions of things both natural and moral ... are certain, unalterable and real in the things themselves, and do not at all depend on the variable opinions, fancies or imaginations of men ...; and also that the mind of man naturally and unavoidably gives its assent, as to natural and geometrical truth, so also to the moral differences of things and to the fitness and reasonableness of the obligation of the everlasting law of righteousness ... [60]

There are three important strands in this passage. One is what may be called 'ethical *objectivism*' – the thesis that moral properties (e.g. the rightness and wrongness of actions) are objectively 'there', or as Clarke puts it, 'real in the things themselves'. The second is a *necessitarian* view of ethical truth: the view that moral principles are 'unalterable' and 'everlasting', possessing the same kind of unavoidable necessity as the principles of geometry. And the third strand is what may be called ethical *apriorism* – the view that ethical principles are arrived at independently of 'any learning or experience in the world' as Clarke puts it. In other words, they are acquired not by empirical investigation but by reason alone; and they must be assented to (Clarke tells us elsewhere) by 'all rational creatures'. [61]

HUME'S CRITIQUE OF ETHICAL RATIONALISM

If we put these three strands of objectivism, necessitarianism and apriorism together, then we have a clear paradigm of ethical rationalism as it stood in the eighteenth century. And, as so often, it is David Hume who provides the rationalist position with its most formidable challenge.

First, he pours scorn on objectivism: the wrongfulness of murder for example cannot, Hume argues, be an objective feature in the action itself ('examine it in all lights and see if you can find the matter of fact or real existence which you call *vice* . . . The vice entirely escapes you so long as you consider the object'). Hume goes on to argue for a form of ethical subjectivism, suggesting that the wrongfulness (or 'viciousness') of murder is simply a matter of a feeling or 'sentiment of disapprobation in your own breast'.[62] Secondly, Hume attacks necessitarianism: moral propositions cannot be based on logically necessary relationships between concepts in the way which happens in mathematics. 'When it is affirmed that two and three are equal to the half of ten, this relation of equality I understand perfectly . . . But when you draw thence a comparison to moral relations, I own that I am altogether at a loss to understand you. A moral action, a crime such as ingratitude, is a complicated object. Does the morality consist in the relation of its parts to each other? How? After what manner?'[63] And finally, Hume attacks the aprioristic thesis that moral principles can be discovered by reason alone. Morality, according to Hume is a matter of passion, sentiment or emotion. We regard an action as 'right' if we have a feeling of approval towards it. Yet reason alone cannot tell us whether to approve or disapprove of something. 'Reason is and ought only to be the slave of the passions, and can never pretend to any other office than to serve and obey them.' We may share or abhor someone's ethical preferences, but there is no way we can demonstrate that they are 'rational' or 'irrational': 'it is not contrary to reason to prefer the destruction of the whole world to the scratching of my finger.'[64]

While not all of Hume's arguments have won universal acceptance, it seems fair to say that his critique of ethical rationalism has remained a dominant force in moral philosophy in our own century. Indeed some theories – like the emotive theory of ethics developed by A. J. Ayer and Charles Stevenson in the 1930s and '40s,[65] follow directly in the Humean tradition by asserting that ethical utterances are expressions of feeling or sentiment rather than propositions expressing rationally decidable claims. But the Humeans have certainly not had it all their own way, and this is due in large part to the enduring vitality of another tradition in ethics which stems from the work of Immanuel Kant.

KANT'S 'CATEGORICAL IMPERATIVE'

In complete contrast to the Humean position sketched above, Kant attempts to defend a rationalistic and objectivist account of morality. In his *Groundwork of the Metaphysics of Morals (Grundlegung zur Metaphysik der Sitten* 1785), Kant asserts that 'everyone must admit that a law has to carry with it absolute necessity if it is to be valid morally'. A moral law must hold 'for all rational beings'; and the ground of obligation must be looked for 'not in the nature of man nor in the circumstances of the world in which he is placed, but solely *a priori*, in the concepts of pure reason'.[66]

Morality is concerned with imperatives or commands, and Kant puts forward a supreme principle of morality which he calls the *categorical imperative*. Most commands ('move that pawn one place forward', or 'have your car serviced every six months') are *hypothetical*; that is, they tell you what you should do *if* you wish to achieve a certain goal (win at chess; prevent the engine seizing up). Such hypothetical commands merely tell us what actions are necessary to achieve a particular purpose, 'and we can always escape from the precept if we abandon the purpose'.[67] But the categorical imperative is 'an unconditional demand which does not leave it open to the will to do the opposite at its discretion'; it is incumbent upon us to obey it no matter what. The single categorical imperative which, for Kant, is the source of all morality is 'act only on that maxim through which you can at the same time will that it should become a universal law' or 'act as if the maxim of your action were to become a universal law of nature'.[68]

Kant provides several examples of how the categorical

imperative works. A sick man in despair may be tempted to take his own life, acting on the maxim that 'from self love I make it my principle to shorten my life if its continuance promises more evil than pleasure'. But according to Kant, one cannot rationally will that the principle of self-love should become a universal law of nature, for 'a system of nature by whose law the very same feeling whose function is to stimulate the furtherance of life should actually destroy life, would contradict itself.' Again, wilfully breaking promises (e.g. securing a loan when one was short of cash by promising to pay the money back, although one knew this to be impossible) could not become a universal law. For if everyone in need supposed he could make any promise he pleased with no intention to perform it, 'it would make promising and the very purpose of promising impossible'.[69] However, these examples are not equally convincing. It is true that one cannot universalize the maxim 'let me break promises whenever it suits me', for if everyone acted on such a maxim the institution of promising would collapse. Hence the 'free-rider' who proposes to take advantage of the institution of promising whenever it suits him, cannot rationally will that his maxim should become a universal law. But it is hard to see how the decision to commit suicide, in the case described by Kant, involves any ultimate 'contradiction'. Even if the decision is taken for purely selfish motives, it is not immediately clear that there is anything intrinsically irrational about an ethic based on egoism, or anything incoherent about universalizing the maxim 'each man for himself'.[70]

One of the most influential moral philosophers of recent times, R. M. Hare, has argued that moral judgements are universalizable in something like Kant's sense. Hare suggests that the force of the universalizability requirement can be seen if, when contemplating treating someone in a selfish or egotistical way, we ask ourselves 'would I be prepared to be treated in this way in similar circumstances?' Now clearly the device of 'putting oneself in other people's shoes' (or adopting the 'golden rule': 'do as you would be done by') captures a great deal of what most people understand by the moral outlook. But the problem remains that a sufficiently determined egoist might well be prepared to universalize his principles without being guilty of any irrationality or inconsistency. Indeed, this is true not just of egoism but of many systems of conduct which most of us would regard as repugnant. A fanatical racist who proposes that someone should be enslaved because he is black might well be prepared to universalize his maxim and propose as a 'universal law of nature' that anyone who is black should be enslaved; and if challenged by being asked 'what if you were black?', he might well reply 'in that case, I should be enslaved too'.[71] Universalizability may indeed be a valuable weapon in moral judgement in so far as it forces people to be aware of just what would be involved if their principles were consistently applied, but by itself it is insufficient to establish that 'immoral' maxims (like those of the egoist or the racist) are ones which no rational creature could accept.

A fundamental difficulty in regarding universalizability as the source of morality is that it appears to be a purely *formal* requirement. It can spell out the implications of a maxim, or the consequences of applying it consistently, but it cannot demonstrate that any maxim is substantively valid 'in itself'. Reasoning must start from somewhere; it must work *from* certain presumptions or premises; and despite Kant's efforts there does not seem any way of showing that we can derive substantive moral laws from objectively valid principles which compel the assent of any rational being. As J. L. Mackie, a recent defender of a subjectivist position in ethics as against the Kantian view, has put it:

Somewhere in the input to [a moral] argument – perhaps in one or more of the premises, perhaps in some part of the form of the argument – there will be something which cannot be objectively validated – some premiss which is not capable of being simply true, some form of argument which is not valid as a matter of general logic, whose authority or cogency is not objective but is constituted by our choosing or deciding to think in a certain way.[72]

ETHICAL NATURALISM

Even if moral principles cannot be discovered *a priori*, by 'pure reason', it still remains possible that they might be derivable from an investigation of certain facts about human nature or the human situation. This approach, which may loosely be termed 'ethical naturalism' is followed by Aristotle in the *Nicomachean Ethics*, where we are offered an account of the good for man which is based on an analysis of man's essential nature and his characteristic 'ergon' or function.[73] During most of our century, however, the prospects for ethical naturalism have looked distinctly dim. There are two main challenges which the ethical naturalist has had to face.

(i) The naturalistic fallacy and the fact-value dichotomy. The first challenge is posed by what has come to be known as the doctrine of the 'naturalistic fallacy'.[74] This doctrine states that any attempt to derive moral or evaluative conclusions from 'natural' (factual or non-evaluative) premises is illegitimate. This is yet another area where the work of Hume has been powerfully influential. For it was Hume who first spotlighted the logical difficulty of deriving a proposition containing an 'ought' from a proposition, or set of propositions, containing merely 'is' statements. 'It seems altogether inconceivable how this new relation [expressed by 'ought'] can be a deduction from others which are entirely different from it.'[75]

Despite some ingenious attempts to bridge this gap between 'is' and 'ought', particularly during the 1960s,[76] the doctrine of the naturalistic fallacy has remained a serious obstacle to the claims of ethical naturalism. Recently however, an increasing number of philosophers have begun to attack the doctrine not so much by attempting to bridge the gap between 'is' and 'ought', as by suggesting that the dichotomy between factual and evaluative statements is untenable in the first place. Such philosophers are strongly influenced by recent developments in the philosophy of science,[77] which have cast doubt on the plausibility of the seemingly common-sense belief that the world consists of neutral 'data' or 'facts' waiting to be perceived. The truth of the matter, according to one critic of the common-sense view, is that, 'we are never neutral even in what we "see" – we must always select, interpret and classify. This is just as true of scientific observers as of ordinary ones'. And the conclusion is that 'facts are never logically isolated from some kind of evaluating'.[78]

But there seems to be a confusion here; for the premise about the need for selection, interpretation and classification simply does not support the conclusion that the facts in question are never logically isolated from some kind of evaluating. It is undoubtedly true that the gathering of data, whether in science or in any other area, is bound to be determined in part by the goals, interests and priorities – in a word values – of the observer. Eskimoes (to employ a hackneyed example) have lots of different words for snow; they see distinctions which no desert-dweller would recognize. And the subtlety of such discriminations no doubt reflects the values of Eskimo society: snow is, naturally enough, very important to them. But it simply does not follow from this that the propositions which the Eskimo asserts are themselves evaluative, or have an evaluative element. It is a mistake to suppose that the values and goals which lead people to investigate a certain class of phenomena somehow 'carry over' into the content of the propositions which they use to describe the phenomena. An investigation into the behaviour of tides may be motivated by mercantile interests, or a passionate belief in the importance of naval superiority; but that patently does not entail that the proposition that high tide on such and such a beach is at such and such a time is somehow covertly, or in any other way, evaluative.

It may be objected here that even if there are some cases where scientific fact is a matter of fairly straightforward measurement, in the great majority of cases the 'facts' will be a matter of more or less complex interpretation ('we always select, interpret and classify'); and it is here that the evaluative inevitably creeps in. However, what seems to follow from the insistence that all or most scientific facts are 'interpreted' rather than 'brute' is that the facts are necessarily *theory-laden*; and this seems a quite different proposition from the proposition that they are value-laden. Let us for the moment assume[79] that there is no neutral observation-language; there are no 'brute facts' which will enable us to decide the issue between two different scientific theories. What follows? Presumably that the observation-statements which are produced to support either theory do not have the status of 'objective' facts; instead they involve an element of interpretation, assessment or whatever. But why should this make them evaluative? Some philosophers have suggested that to adopt a set of descriptive expressions is 'already to choose an attitude'.[80] But this is ambiguous. To interpret a given photographic plate as evidence of a stellar red shift is, it may be allowed, to adopt a certain 'attitude' to it, in the sense that what is involved is a complex process of appraisal, assessment, judgement, estimation, computation, comparison and so forth – many of which activities can only be performed in the context of an elaborate theoretical model. But to concede that the scientist must take up an attitude in this interesting but relatively innocent sense is not at all to say that he must take up an evaluative stance, if this is taken to mean that there must necessarily be some element of approval, or disapproval, or favourable or unfavourable grading embedded into the content of his assertions.

The upshot is that recent work in the philosophy of science about the difficulty of isolating 'neutral' facts is not by itself sufficient to undermine the Humean distinction between 'is' and 'ought', between description and evaluation. And that distinction therefore remains a serious obstacle to the attempt to found a system of ethics upon a descriptive account of human nature.

(ii) The challenge of existentialism. The second major challenge to naturalism arises as follows. If an ethical system is

to be based on an analysis of human nature, there must be an identifiable human nature or essence: there must be a characteristic set of properties which define our essential nature as human beings. Thus, for Aristotle, man's essential characteristic is his rationality, and human fulfilment must therefore involve the exercise and development of this attribute. A recent 'neo-naturalist', Mary Midgley, follows a similar strategy, and maintains that there are certain fundamental characteristics, which are true of us *qua* human beings – certain 'deep structural constituents of our characters': 'our basic repertoire of wants is given. We are not free to create or annihilate wants . . . No human being can possibly find himself going out to shop for values for the first time.'[81]

Yet this notion of a fundamental human essence that constrains our ethical choice is precisely what has been challenged by the existentialist movement in philosophy, which has achieved a widespread following in the last few decades mainly as a result of the work of Jean-Paul Sartre. The Sartrean slogan 'existence precedes essence' means in effect that for human beings there is no fixed, determined 'essence' or 'nature' which limits our freedom. A mere thing, or *être en soi*, can only do what is in its nature to do; a machine, or even an animal, is in the position of existing within the framework of a predetermined set of essential dispositions and responses. But for a human being, an *être pour soi*, existence comes first; that is, we find ourselves here in the world faced with the choice of how to live – there are no 'givens'. The belief in 'human nature' as a limiting factor which exists prior to our choice is a case of 'bad faith'; our choice is absolutely free and unrestricted by any prior constraints.[82]

If the contrast between the naturalist and the existentialist is put as starkly as this, then it may at first sight appear that it is the naturalist position which is robustly realistic and backed by common sense, while the existentialist claim belongs to the world of fantasy. The existentialist seems to be talking as if a human being is a pure mind who creates his future *ex nihilo*. Yet it can hardly be denied that first of all, man is a physical, three-dimensional being, subject, like any other such being, to innumerable physical constraints, such as the law of gravity. Second, and more importantly, he is an *animal* – a warm-blooded animal with a specific genetic inheritance. All this seems so straightforward and obvious as to make the Sartrean refusal to acknowledge any limitation on our freedom seem either perverse or fatuous.

However, to leave the matter thus is to miss the point of the existentialist rejection of the idea of human nature or essence. Statements about essences license universal necessary truths.[83] All water must evaporate when heated above 100 degrees Celsius at a certain pressure: it is of the nature or essence of water to do so. Similarly, all cows, placed in a field under suitable conditions, are bound to eat grass – that is their nature. But – and here is the existentialist's point – there are no such universal predictions that can validly be made about human beings. Of course, if you push someone over a cliff, he will fall; but that is true of him *qua* physical object, not *qua* person. Of course, if you deprive him of food or air he will die; but that is true of him *qua* animal. But in so far as he is a human being there is, quite literally, nothing that can be safely predicted. In the case of humans, there are no universal statements that can be made comparable to such statements as 'all cows eat grass'. Any supposed feature which allegedly defines man's essence is subject to counter-examples. 'Man is a social animal': but there are hermits who live in total isolation. 'Man is philoprogenitive': but there are many who deliberately decide against having children. 'Man is rational': yet D. H. Lawrence tells us that the life of reason is 'dead' – without vigour or meaning. In short, any feature or activity proposed as definitive of the nature or essence of man can be denied by a human agent, in the sense that it is open to him to conduct his life without reference to that feature or activity. This is the kernel of truth in the existentialist slogan 'existence precedes essence', and the truth behind the (misleading) insistence on 'total freedom'.

If this is right, then it has important implications for the naturalist programme. Starting from an analysis of the essential nature of cows, we can indeed draw conclusions about the good for cows. All cows eat grass; and it is in the nature of cows to flourish and prosper when placed in lush meadows with plenty of space, sunshine, fresh air, and so on. But there is no parallel argument which can get us to valid conclusions about man's *eudaimonia* or fulfilment. That is, there is no set of physical, psychological or sociological facts such that any rational person who accepts them is logically bound to reach certain evaluations about how life should be lived. Part of the reason for this is that flourishing or 'the good' for plants or animals is defined straightforwardly in terms of physical survival, growth, health and procreation. Hence it is just obvious that a life of captivity is not a good life for a panda: the wretched animals won't eat, or develop physiological disorders, or lose their sexual desires. But a man in captivity can still practise that highest Aristotelian virtue – *theoria*; according to the Buddhists, a man at the point of starvation may achieve *nirvana*; and, according to the sayings of Jesus, being 'reviled and persecuted' can be an occasion for 'blessedness'. The point of referring to these strange but nevertheless highly respected conceptions of human *eudaimonia* is not to advocate them, but simply to illustrate the enormous variety in possible and indeed respectably held conceptions of the good for man: human *eudaimonia*, unlike that of any other species, is an indeterminate concept which can be filled in with an indefinite number of different and widely divergent blueprints.[84] And if this is right then the attempt to derive an objectively valid ethical system from an analysis of 'human nature' is doomed to failure.

REASON IN ETHICS

If the various arguments put forward above are correct, then one must be highly pessimistic about the prospects for rationalism in ethics, i.e. the attempt to construct a rational and objectively valid set of ethical principles either *a priori* or on the basis of facts about human nature. But the reader should be warned against inferring from this that there is no place for *reason* in ethics. For one thing, even if there is no objective way of establishing the goals or ends of the good life, reason will always have a vital role to play in the calculation of the best means for achieving whatever goals we happen to select. A second important consideration is that the requirements of logic and consistency apply to ethical language just as they do in any other area. Thus to call an action 'X' *right* is to be logically committed to calling any other action 'Y' right if it resembles X in all relevant respects. As we have seen in discussing Hare, this notion of consistency cannot establish that racism, for example, is intrinsically irrational. But by skilful use of the consistency requirement, it may nevertheless be possible to convince people that they can produce no logically relevant reasons why groups such as blacks or women should be treated differently from any other members of the community.

Reason then has a vital role to play in ethics both in enabling us to work out how to realize our goals, and in eliminating inconsistencies and muddles from our moral outlook. But at the end of the day it appears that there will remain a fundamental limitation on the scope of reason in the realm of ethics as opposed, say, to natural science. In science we are aiming to provide a progressively clearer account of the world as it really is.[85] In ethics, there is no such unifying goal; and even when reason has done its work in devising optimum strategies for achieving our goals and eliminating inconsistencies, there will remain a variety of equally viable and equally consistent visions of the good life, and no reason to think (as we do think in science) that further empirical evidence or further rational reflection will enable us to make an objective decision as to which vision is preferable.

F. RATIONALISM, EMPIRICISM AND SCIENTIFIC METHOD

KARL POPPER AND FALSIFIABILITY

We saw in earlier chapters that the thought of many of the rationalists (Spinoza is the classic example here) was strongly influenced by a *deductive* model of knowledge. Propositions are deduced in a precise, step by step fashion from first principles, and their truth is guaranteed by the fact that they follow necessarily from those principles. The standard empiricist criticism of this model is that logical deduction will only tell us what follows from what; if we want to find out what is actually the case, we will need to employ not deduction but observation. Thus the empiricist typically argues that scientific laws must be established not deductively but *inductively*: the scientist infers general truths from particular observations and experiments. However, as emerged in our discussion of positivism,[86] there is a serious problem with the inductivist account of science: scientific observations and experiments must necessarily be limited to a finite number of instances; yet how is a finite number of observations supposed to establish the truth of a general law which is to be applicable universally – to all cases past, present and future? It is precisely this difficulty that Karl Popper's theory of the logic of science aimed to obviate.

Although Karl Popper (born 1902) was associated with members of the Vienna Circle during the 1920s, he became highly critical of many of their doctrines, and his *Logic of Scientific Discovery (Logik der Forschung*, 1934) marks a decisive break with the verificationism of the positivists. Popper concluded at an early stage that the problem of induction was insoluble; the truth of scientific laws could never be established by a finite number of observations. But Popper's revolutionary suggestion was that the long unsolved 'problem of induction' was irrelevant to the questions of scientific knowledge. Popper doubted whether scientists in fact ever arrived at theories by 'inducing' general laws from particular observations; but he argued that in any case the question of how scientists manage to arrive at their theories is a matter for psychology, not logic. There is no logical path leading from observation to scientific laws. Scientists may arrive at their theories in a variety of ways, perhaps, as Einstein suggested, by a leap of creative insight which cannot logically be mapped.[87] What is important, however, is not how the theories are arrived at, but the question of how the theories are to be tested, once proposed. And here Popper argues that strictly logical, deductive reasoning is applicable. Scientific theories cannot logically be guaranteed to be true, but they are logically capable of being proved false; for by the logical principle known as *modus tollens*, if theory T implies, as a deductive consequence, observation statement O, then if it is the case that O is false, then T must be false. As Popper put it: 'The falsification of or refutation of theories through the falsification or refutation of their deductive consequences is, clearly, a deductive inference (*modus tollens*).'[88] The principle of falsifiability is, for Popper, the essence of the logic of science. Science proceeds (in the words of the title of one of Popper's later books) by 'conjectures and refutations'. A theory is put forward as a tentative hypothesis; the consequences deduced from it are tested against experience; if the observations actually made are inconsistent with those predicted by the theory, then the theory is refuted and the way is open for a new conjecture.

Popper thus rejected the ruling empiricist dogma of verificationism and proposed in its place the principle of falsifiability – though he regarded this not as a criterion of meaningfulness but as a principle of demarcation which marks off genuine scientific theories from pseudo-science. And the logic of falsification was characterized in terms of strictly deductive reasoning.

If one contrasts this 'deductivism' (the label is Popper's own choice[89]) with the inductivist approach of say, Francis Bacon or J. S. Mill, then it might seem appropriate to place Popper in the rationalist camp rather than with the empiricists. But in one important respect such a classification would be misleading. One strand in rationalism is, as we have seen, the belief in the possibility of *a priori* knowledge; yet Popper insists on a paramount role for *a posteriori*, empirical observation in the testing of scientific theories. To be a genuine contribution to scientific knowledge a theory must, for Popper, 'stick its neck out' and expose itself to the risk of empirical falsification. Our observations cannot guarantee the truth of scientific theories but they can refute them, and any theory which does not expose itself to the risk of empirical refutation does not deserve to be called a contribution to science.

What emerges from these comments is that Popper cannot safely be placed on either side of the rationalist/ empiricist dichotomy. Indeed, it should by now be clear that this dichotomy should never be applied too rigidly: to divide philosophers into two neat, mutually exclusive piles of this sort is to allow a zeal for tidy-mindedness to distort the truth. Our earlier discussions of Aristotle, Descartes and Kant have already provided examples of thinkers whose ideas cannot without distortion be forced into one of two neat pigeon-holes labelled respectively 'empiricism' and 'rationalism'.[90] Part of the reason for this is that there is no one simple, official doctrine that defines 'rationalism'; rather, there are a number of overlapping and mutually reinforcing trends that make up what is commonly called the rationalist tradition. Popper belongs to that tradition in so far as he believes in the creative power of the mind in some sense to 'go beyond' direct observation, in its attempts to reach the truth. But he is an empiricist in so far as he believes that any such leaps of 'creative intuition' can only qualify as genuine contributions to science if they can be made to yield consequences which can be brought to the bar of empirical observation and tested against experience.

THE RECENT REVOLUTION IN THE PHILOSOPHY OF SCIENCE

For Popper, it is the deductive structures of logic that give science its rationality, while it is the ability to yield consequences that may conflict with actual experience that gives science its objective status. In the last two decades, however, there has been a revolution in the philosophy of science that has cast considerable doubt both on the rationality of the scientific enterprise, and its claims to objectivity. The thinkers discussed so far in this book, while not always neatly classifiable in terms of the rationalist/empiricist distinction, can at least be seen as contributing to a continuing dialogue in which, for example, Spinoza's deductive, *a priori* account of substance, and Hume's reduction of causation to observed regularities, may be seen as representing two extremes. But the recent revolution in the philosophy of science is not so much a further development of the dialogue as an abrupt breaking off: in its extreme form it rejects both the rationalist and the empiricist models of knowledge as fundamentally misguided.

The two central figures in this new approach are Thomas Kuhn and Paul Feyerabend, whose landmark publications (Kuhn's book *The Structure of Scientific Revolutions* and Feyerabend's article 'Explanation, Reduction and Empiricism'), both appeared in 1962. Both writers followed Popper in rejecting the empiricist model of the scientist as 'collecting facts' or gradually accumulating knowledge through observation and experiment. But they rejected the Popperian notion that theories can be falsified by having their consequences checked against experience. Kuhn argued that once a given explanatory theory or model becomes dominant in a scientific community, scientists will refuse to allow it to be falsified by anomalous results. The entrenched ruling models or 'paradigms' that dominate the thought of a scientific community enjoy a kind of special protection: 'once it has achieved the status of a paradigm, a scientific theory is declared invalid only if an alternative is available to take its place.'[91] Normal science is a matter of routine puzzle-solving carried on within the terms of the ruling paradigm. Only in periods of scientific crisis, when anomalous results become unmanageable and an alternative paradigm presents itself, will a fundamental paradigm shift or revolution in scientific thinking occur.

A Popperian might well reply to this that the principle of falsifiability is intended as a logical standard or norm which a scientific theory *ought* to measure up to; Popper's theory does not, and need not, claim that scientists always operate in a way which in fact measures up to that standard. But the arguments of Kuhn and Feyerabend are not confined to the issue of how scientists actually operate. First of all, they cast doubt on the whole notion that the consequences of a theory can be tested against the facts. There is, they maintain, no sharp distinction between the statements of theory and the reports of observation. A so-called 'observation report' may be heavily laden with theory (as when the interpretation of a given reading involves complex theoretical assumptions and/or calculations). And it follows from this that the idea that a theory can always be tested against a neutrally described set of 'empirical facts', and discarded if it does not fit them, is suspect. Secondly, when theories *are* overthrown, this is not, according to Kuhn, a matter of the new theory improving on the old one by giving a better account of the hitherto recalcitrant data. Rather, there is a 'gestalt-switch': the world is suddenly viewed through new conceptual spectacles. The new paradigm and its associated theory generate new 'data' – they provide us with a radically different way of seeing things. Thus astronomers after the Copernican revolution 'lived in a different world'.[92] Third, and most crucial, both Kuhn and Feyerabend independently arrived at the conclusion that different scientific theories are 'incommensurable'. If observations depend on theory, and theory in some sense determines how we read 'the world', then it seems that there will be no rational and objective way of deciding between two differing scientific theories. There will be no common basis from which we can make a neutral and objective evaluation of which theory is preferable. This has come to be known as the 'incommensurability thesis'. As Kuhn puts it, 'the competition between paradigms is not the sort of battle that can be resolved by proofs'.[93]

If we take the three main elements in the view of science just sketched, viz. (i) the dependence of observation on theory, (ii) the notion of scientific change as a 'paradigm-shift' involving a gestalt-switch, and (iii) the thesis of the incommensurability of differing theories, then together they present a powerful challenge to the claims to objectivity of any scientific or philosophic world-view. And the question arises as to whether we can say with any confidence that our own contemporary scientific culture represents an advance on the work of previous systems of thought. While it may be possible to chart and describe the course of science from an historical or sociological point of view, it begins to look as if there will be no objective reason for saying that at any given stage science is nearer 'the truth' than at any other. In Feyerabend, this thought is carried to its ultimate conclusion: modern Western science is simply a 'dominant ideology'; it is one tradition among many, with no special claim to our acceptance. 'One must read ideologies like fairy tales which have . . . interesting things to say but which also contain wicked lies . . . Scientific "facts" are taught at a very early age in the very same manner in which religious "facts" were taught only a century ago.' The result of all this (though many philosophers, including Kuhn himself in his later writings, have been reluctant to go the whole way with Feyerabend) is an extreme form of epistemological relativism (some would say 'anarchism') in which not only theories themselves, but also the very methodological standards in terms of which they are evaluated, lose any plausible claim to objective correctness.[94]

RATIONALISM AND RELATIVISM

What are the implications for rationalism of these developments? One important and disturbing point should already be apparent. If the notion of 'objective reality' is suspect, if 'truth' has no application except within the context of a particular world-view, and there is no neutral way of comparing world-views, then the conception of philosophy which is typically found in the great rationalist thinkers will be fatally undermined. According to Plato, the job of the philosopher is to uncover the world of eternal realities, the Forms, which exist independently of human beings. According to Descartes, the human mind has the power to form 'clear and distinct' ideas – ideas which represent what is objectively real and true. It is central to these conceptions of philosophy that the human mind is capable of, indeed is a reliable instrument for, uncovering the true structure of reality (in Descartes' words 'a reliable mind was God's gift to me').[95] Yet if the incommensurability thesis is right, it seems that we will have to abandon this conception of philosophical inquiry as an attempt to uncover the 'objective truth'.

This, according to the conclusion reached by Richard Rorty in his much acclaimed *Philosophy and the Mirror of Nature* (1980), is precisely what we should do. We must, Rorty argues, abandon the conception of philosophical knowledge held, among others, by Plato and Descartes, which asserts 'that the universe is made up . . . of simple, clearly and distinctly knowable things, knowledge of whose essence provides the master-vocabulary which permits commensuration of all discourses.'[96] Rorty's thesis is that there is something wrong with the view that philosophy can construct some canonical language which 'limns the true and ultimate structure of reality'. Traditional 'foundational epistemology', Rorty argues, 'proceeds on the assumption that all contributions to a given discourse are commensurable – i.e. can be brought under a set of rules which will tell us how rational agreement can be reached or what would settle the issue on every point where statements seem to conflict.'

Rejecting this assumption, Rorty also rejects the view of the philosopher as a kind of 'cultural overseer who knows everyone's common ground'.[97] In place of the traditional epistemology, Rorty proposes that philosophy should develop into 'hermeneutics'; that is, instead of trying to establish the 'foundations of all knowledge', it should acknowledge that all understanding must operate *within* a given conceptual framework. The hermeneutic philosopher can offer interpretation and analysis by immersing himself in a given world-view, but he cannot pass 'objective' judgement on it, from the outside as it were. 'The application of honorifics such as "objective" is never anything more than an expression of the presence of, or the hope for, agreement among inquirers'; we need to give up the idea that 'our criteria of successful inquiry are not just *our* criteria, but also the *right* criteria, nature's criteria, the criteria which will lead us to the *truth*'.[98]

PROBLEMS WITH RELATIVISM

Rorty's strictures, like those of Feyerabend, do not, of course, apply only to those philosophers who are normally called 'rationalists'. If the incommensurability thesis is correct, then there is no neutral observation language which is capable of recording 'the facts', and it will follow that empiricist approaches to knowledge are equally under attack; neither the standard empiricist notion of verification by the senses, nor the more sophisticated Popperian notion of empirical falsifiability will be able to justify any claims to ultimate objectivity. What is threatened is not just rationalism in the technical sense (the sense in which Spinoza and Leibniz are rationalists), but rationalism in the wider sense of a commitment to rationality as a universal standard for all human discourse.[99] For the relativist claims that there are no independently valid standards which determine what makes a belief rational. What counts as a 'good reason' for holding a belief will vary from culture to culture, and there is no objective reason for preferring any one set of standards.

But this in turn suggests that relativism may have overreached itself. If the notions like meaning and truth can only be understood from within a given conceptual framework, then it seems impossible for the relativist to argue that his criticisms of traditional epistemology are in any strong sense *justified* or *correct*. What we seem to have is two rival conceptions of philosophical inquiry: the traditional approach, which sees philosophy as 'limning the structure of reality', and the relativist view which insists that meaning and truth are relative to a given conceptual scheme. But now, on pain of contradicting his relativist thesis, the relativist cannot argue that the traditional view is objectively *mistaken*.[100] Moreover, if there are no objectively rational reasons for adopting any given theory, then this perforce applies to relativism itself.

Does this mean that relativism is self-refuting? One is reminded here of the spectacularly self-destructive claim of a leading British Freudian that 'all human judgements, and even reason itself, are but the tools of the unconscious; and such seemingly acute convictions which an intelligent person possesses are but the inevitable effects of the causes which lie buried in the unconscious levels of his psyche'.[101] The claim evidently destroys itself because if *all* judgements are determined by unconscious forces, and this makes them in some sense suspect, then this must apply to the judgements of the Freudian himself. And similarly, in the present case, if *all* truth is relative to a given world-view, and cannot claim objective 'correctness', then this must apply to the 'truths' which the relativist himself claims to propound. Some relativists, however, are prepared to accept this consequence; thus Rorty readily admits that there is no way in which to 'argue' the issue of whether objective rationality has a place in science. 'If there is no common ground, all we can do is to show how the other side looks from our point of view.'[102] This manoeuvre does rescue relativism from being obviously self-stultifying, but it lumbers the relativist with the disquieting concession that he cannot offer any decisive reasons for his position – any reasons which ought to convince a non-relativist.[103]

In spite of this difficulty, the relativist does present rationalism with a serious challenge – the challenge of making sense of the claim that philosophy can somehow soar above the limits of the conceptual apparatus of a given culture, and reach up to some 'absolute' truth. Is not this aspiration an absurdly ambitious – perhaps incoherent – one?

In one way, there is nothing new about the problem. We have seen an analogous kind of difficulty arise in connection with the Cartesian belief in the reliability of the mind as an instrument for uncovering reality. My mind is reliable, says Descartes, because it is bestowed on me by God; yet I must assume in advance that it is reliable if I am to establish a valid proof of God's existence.[104] There does not seem to be any way out of the circle. Reason cannot, surely, be its own guarantor; and if it cannot be its own guarantor, then it cannot guarantee the objectivity of its results.

THE PROSPECTS FOR RATIONALISM

A possible escape route for the rationalist here would be to argue that there are certain universal principles of reasoning which are not just true relative to a given world-view, but which are presupposed in any discourse whatsoever. One such principle (which relativists often seem anxious to avoid discussing) is the principle of non-contradiction, the principle that a given proposition and its denial cannot both be simultaneously true. (This corresponds with the theorem '$-(P \& -P)$', or 'it is not the case that both P and not P'). Some extreme relativists have tried to suggest that logical theory, like any other theory, operates within, and is a part of, the ruling ideology of a given culture. Thus Peter Winch, in his celebrated *The Idea of a Social Science* declares 'the criteria of logic are not a direct gift from God but arise out of and are only intelligible in the context of ways of living and modes of social life'.[105] But the principle of non-contradiction clearly transcends the limits of this or that cultural or scientific system; rather it defines what is to count as a system of thought in the first place. A system which dispensed with the principle of non-contradiction would allow anything whatsoever to be asserted; and this means it would not be an 'alternative system' – it would not be a system at all.

The principle of non-contradiction, then, provides at least one example of a proposition that is 'neutral'; it gives us an inter-cultural standpoint for the kind of objective assessment that can go beyond the particularities of history and geography. What is more, it is a principle with practical applications. If it is necessarily true that '$-(P \& -P)$', then it follows that an inconsistent statement, a proposition of the form '$P \& -P$', is, necessarily, false. And it follows from this that a scientific or philosophical system which contains inconsistencies must, however widely it is accepted, contain some element of falsity.

There may well be other kinds of discourse (apart from the laws of logic) that achieve the kind of neutrality that the relativist claims is impossible. 'This stuff in the tube is now turning red' is surely the kind of statement whose truth is uninfected by any particular theoretical assumption, ideological stance, or ruling paradigm. And this suggests the kind of strategy that might be used to defend the notions of rationality and objectivity against the attacks of the relativist. It may be possible to establish an intercultural core of objective truths based on the universal constraints of logic, coupled with the simple non-theoretical beliefs which are based on our ordinary perceptual experience. (Many relativists would challenge these notions of 'ordinary perceptual experience' and 'simple non-theoretical beliefs'; but the most promising line for the rationalist to take here seems to be to concentrate on paradigm cases like 'this is turning red' or 'this pointer is moving to the left'.[106])

Even if the rationalist can establish such a 'bridge-head' of logic plus low-level perceptual beliefs, the problem remains – and it is a formidable one – of showing how the constraints so far established are strong enough and precise enough to enable us to determine that a given theory is 'an advance on' or 'nearer the truth than' its predecessor. But however formidable the task, it cannot, surely, be a hopeless one. For it is as well to remind ourselves of some comfortable and prosaic facts – even though such a reminder will of course be condemned by the relativist as question-begging. There really *is* an objective world 'out there'; the bodies which we call the sun and the planets really are moving around, quite independently of anything we think or believe, and will continue to do so long after we are gone; and we really do know more, much more, about them today than we did 500 years ago.

And what, after all, is so monstrous in the idea that the philosopher or the scientist can construct a system that will somehow mirror or reflect reality? For are we not a part of the universe? And what, then, is so strange in the idea that our minds are suitably structured instruments for understanding it? The notion that we can attain to some sort of 'absolute' truth is of course wrong: we are finite beings and reality, if not infinite, is certainly indefinitely larger than anything which our finite minds can grasp. But if we cannot construct a flawless mirror to reflect the vast and complex structure of reality, then at least we may be able to discern some part of its structure, albeit through a glass that is necessarily murky and distorted. The perfect fit envisaged by Descartes' 'clear and distinct ideas' may be wildly optimistic. But that is no reason to abandon the notion of objective reality, or to give up the struggle to make our view of it progressively clearer, more comprehensive and more accurate.

NOTES

1. Michael Rosen, 'Hegel' in Wintle [97].
2. *My Philosophical Development* [101] p.62.
3. The leading American Hegelian of this period was the Harvard philosopher Josiah Royce (1855–1916).
4. See MacIntyre, *Hegel: A Collection of Critical Essays* [96]. p.vii.
5. 'Don't turn Hegelian and lose yourself in perfumed dreams – the world will never get on unless a few people at least will limit themselves to believing what has been proved and keep clear the distinction between what we really know and

what we don't' (Logan Pearsall Smith quoted in Russell [5] Vol. I, p.94.

6. [94] p.538.
7. J. N. Findlay, 'The Contemporary Relevance of Hegel' in MacIntyre [96] p.16.
8. See above, Ch.2, p.24.
9. See above, Ch.4, pp.74–6.
10. *Phänomenologie des Geistes* [89] section 110 (cited in MacIntyre [96] p.166). By '*bloss Gemeinte*' (literally 'simply meant'), Hegel suggests that we may think we 'mean something' when we point to a sensory datum, but there is nothing that can be coherently expressed in language.
11. Charles Taylor, 'The Opening Arguments of the Phenomenology' in MacIntyre [96] pp.174–5. My exegesis of Hegel at this point is heavily indebted to Taylor's lucid reconstruction of Hegel's often tortuous and obscure argument.
12. See above Ch.3, pp.42–3.
13. See above, Ch.4, pp.84–7.
14. See above, Ch.1, pp.4–5.
15. *Conversation with Burman* [35] pp.12, 68. For Hegel's views on the place of 'traditional' principles of logic, see the additions to *Encyclopaedia*, Section 80 [88] [90].
16. *Language, Truth and Logic* [107] p.36. For Bradley, see above, p.93.
17. Ayer [107] p.73.
18. *The Problems of Philosophy* (1912) [99] pp.12, 51.
19. According to Russell, 'wherever possible; logical constructions are to be substituted for inferred entities'. Russell called this the 'supreme maxim in scientific philosophising'. *Mysticism and Logic* [100] p.155.
20. 'The Relation of Sense-Data to Physics' (1914) repr, in [101] p.105. It should be noted that Russell later abandoned his theory of sense-data. See [101] Ch.IX; also Pears [102] Ch.3.
21. *Tractatus* [104] Prop.5.
22. *Ibid.*, 4.001.
23. *Ibid.*, 6.41.
24. *Ibid.*, 6.1.
25. *Ibid.*, 6.53.
26. Ayer [107] pp.34–5.
27. See above, Ch.2, pp.17–19, Ch.3, p.38ff.
28. *Tractatus*, 4.461.
29. Ayer [107] pp.87, 92.
30. From '*Die Wende der Philosophie*', trans. in *Logical Positivism* [108] p.59.
31. Some positivists suggested that the principle was an 'explication' of all that could plausibly be meant by the term

'meaningful'. See G. Hempel, 'The Empiricist Criterion of Meaning' in [108].

32. Cf. Ayer, *Language, Truth and Logic* [107], Introduction to second edition.

33. Kant defines an analytic proposition slightly differently, in terms of the 'containedness' of the predicate within the subject. See above, p.83.

34. 'Two dogmas of empiricism' (1951); repr. in [110].

35. *Ibid.*, p.42.

36. *Ibid.*

37. *Ibid.*, p.44. See [111] and [112] for Quine's later writings, where some of the claims made in 'Two dogmas' underwent significant revision.

38. *First Enquiry* [73] Section IV, part (i). See above, Ch.4, p.84.

39. [114] p.138 (slightly modified).

40. See above, Ch.2, pp.28–30.

41. [114] p.138 (italics original).

42. *Ibid.*, p.136.

43. *Ibid.*, p.125.

44. For a survey of some of the problems, see Platts [115] Ch.6, Schwartz [116] and Putnam [117].

45. [114] p.138 (slightly modified; italics original).

46. Hook [122] p.x.

47. See above, Ch.4, pp.71–6.

48. Skinner's *Verbal Behaviour* [121] is the subject of a scathing review by Chomsky in *Language*, Vol.35, (1959).

49. 'Recent Contributions to the Theory of Innate Ideas' (1967) repr. in [120] p.123.

50. *Ibid.*, p.124.

51. Cf. *Language and Mind* [118] p.25.

52. [120] p.129.

53. See above, Ch.2, p.26.

54. *Fifth Objections and Replies* (1641); [31] VII, 382; [33] II, 227.

55. For Leibniz see above, Ch.4, p.76. Chomsky cites Leibniz in [120] p.130.

56. Letter to Newcastle 23 November 1646 in *Descartes' Philosophical Letters* [34] p.207.

57. 'Knowledge of Language' (1969), [119].

58. [118] p.22.

59. For a brief survey of some of the empirical research see Lyons [124]; for further philosophical discussion see Hook [122] and Hacking [123], p.57ff. On the question of whether language is 'species-specific', it should be noted that recent research, has suggested that Chimpanzees, at least, may have some degree of linguistic competence.

60. *A Discourse concerning the Unchangeable Obligations of Natural Religion* (1706) repr. in Raphael [126] para. 235.

61. *Ibid.*, para. 233.

62. David Hume, *A Treatise of Human Nature* (1739–40) [72], Bk.III, Part 1, section i.

63. *Enquiry concerning the Principles of Morals* (1751) [127] Appendix 1.

64. *Treatise* [72], Bk. II, Part 3, section ii.

65. See Ayer [107] Ch.6; Charles Stevenson *Ethics and Language* [129] and Urmson [130].

66. p. vi of second edition; translated in Paton [128], p.55.

67. *Ibid.*, p.55.

68. *Ibid.*, p.84.

69. *Ibid.*, p.85.

70. Kant however argues that the rational egoist must recognize that he may one day need the help of others, so he cannot rationally will that egoism become a universal law [128] p.86. For further discussion of Kant's examples see Walker [85] Ch. XI.

71. R. M. Hare's views on universalizability are contained in [131] and [132]. For 'fanaticism' see [131] Ch.9 and [132] Ch.10.

72. *Ethics* [133] p.30. For a contrasting view see Bambrough *Moral Scepticism and Moral Knowledge* [134].

73. *Nicomachean Ethics* [24] Bk.I, Ch.7.

74. This term was first used by G. E. Moore in *Principia Ethica* [135]; but there are certain complications in Moore's account which Hume's treatment (discussed below) avoids.

75. *Treatise* [72] Bk. III, Part 1, section i.

76. Cf. J. Searle 'How to derive "ought" from "is"' *Phil. Review* (1964). Searle's paper, and some searching criticisms of it, are printed in Hudson [136].

77. These developments will be looked at in more detail in section F, below.

78. Midgley, *Beast and Man* [137] p.178.

79. Following the arguments of Thomas Kuhn; see above, p.144ff.

80. Cf. Rorty, *Philosophy and the Mirror of Nature* [151] 364.

81. Midgley [137] pp.182–3.

82. Cf. *L'Etre et le Néant* (1943) [139], Part I, Ch.2 and Part IV, Ch.1.

83. For whether this necessity is 'real' or only 'verbal necessity', see above, section C, pp.117–20.

84. The point is developed further in my 'Neonaturalism and its pitfalls' [138].

85. For this (somewhat unfashionable) view of natural science, see above, section F, p.146–52ff.

86. See above, p.109ff.
87. Popper [143] p.32.
88. Popper [144] p.79.
89. [143] p.30.
90. See above, Ch. 1 p.9ff; Ch. 2 p.26–31; Ch. 3 pp.44–7; Ch. 4, pp.84–6.
91. Kuhn [145] p.77. Cf. Feyerabend [146].
92. Kuhn [145], p.117.
93. *Ibid.*, p.148.
94. Quotation from Paul Feyerabend 'How to defend society against science', *Radical Philosophy* Vol. 2 (1975), repr. in Hacking [147]. Feyerabend prefers to describe himself as a 'realist' (albeit a sceptical one) rather than a relativist, but many commentators doubt whether any plausible version of realism can be accommodated within Feyerabend's thought. See Papineau [150]. For Kuhn's later writings see [148].
95. *Conversation with Burman* [35] p.5.
96. Rorty [151], p.357.
97. *Ibid.*, pp. 300 316, 317.
98. *Ibid.*, pp. 355, 299.
99. See above, Ch.1, pp.2–7.
100. The relativist might, however, try to argue that the traditional programme is incoherent or impossible in terms of its own stated criteria for success. See Hollis & Lukes [156].
101. Berg *Deep Analysis* [152] p.190, quoted in Flew [153].
102. Rorty [151], pp.364–5.
103. For more on the self-refutation argument see Hesse [154], Hollis & Lukes [156].
104. See above, Ch. 3 pp.42–3.
105. [155] p.100.
106. For further discussion of the complex problems involved here, see Hollis & Lukes [156], Newton-Smith [157].

BIBLIOGRAPHY

Note: References to English translations of philosophical works originally written in Greek, Latin, French or German are given below for the reader's convenience, but when quoting passages in the text I have sometimes made emendations or substituted translations of my own.

CHAPTER 1

Concise accounts of some of the concepts ('*a priori*', 'empirical', etc.) introduced in this chapter may be found in:

[1] Flew, A. (ed.) *A Dictionary of Philosophy* (London: Pan Books, 1979).

A much more detailed and extensive reference work is:

[2] Edwards, P. (ed.) *Encyclopaedia of Philosophy* (New York: Macmillan, 1967).

For Nietzsche's views see:

[3] Nietzsche, F. *Die Götzen-Dämmerung (The Twilight of the Gods)*, 1889, translated in Kaufmann, W., *The Portable Nietzsche* (New York: Viking, 1954).

For a more sympathetic view of Nietzsche's glorification of Dionysus, see:

[4] Kaufmann, W. *Nietzsche, Philosopher, Psychologist, Antichrist* (Princeton: Princeton University Press, 1950), Ch.4.

Russell's comment is quoted from:

[5] Russell, B. *The Autobiography of Bertrand Russell* (London: Allen & Unwin, 1968), Vol.II, p.22.

Bacon's *Cogitata et Visa* appears in:

[6] Spedding, J. & Ellis, R. E. (eds.) *The Works of Francis Bacon* (London: Longmans, 1887), Vol.III.

A concise account of Francis Bacon's ideas may be found in:

[7] Quinton, A. *Bacon* (Oxford: Oxford University Press, 1980).

Wittgenstein's discussion of 'overlapping and criss-crossing' is in:

[8] Wittgenstein, L. *Philosophical Investigations (Philosophische Untersuchungen)* 1953. tr. Anscombe, G. E. M. (New York: Macmillan, 1958) Part I, sections 60 ff.

See also the notion of 'open texture' in:

[9] Waismann, F. *Philosophical Papers*, (ed.) McGuinness, B. (Dordrecht: Reidel, 1977).

CHAPTER 2

Note: Works of Plato and Aristotle are referred to by means of standard marginal references which are common to all editions.

PLATO

Many good English translations of Plato are available, including:

[10] Cornford, F. M. *Plato's Theory of Knowledge* (London: Routledge, 1960), which contains the *Theaetetus*.

[11] Lee, H. P. D. *Plato's Republic* (Harmondsworth: Penguin, 1955). Another translation of the *Republic* by F. M. Cornford is published by O.U.P. (1941).

[12] Vlastos, G. *Plato: Protagoras* (New York: Bobbs Merrill, 1956).

[13] Sesonske, A. & Fleming, N. *Plato's Meno* (Belmont: Wadsworth, 1965).

[14] Taylor, A. E. *Plato: The Laws* (London: Dent, 1960).

[15] Tredennick, H. (tr.) *Plato, The Last Days of Socrates* (Harmondsworth: Penguin, rev. 1969). This volume contains the *Euthyphro, Apology, Crito* and *Phaedo*.

Bibliography

An excellent introduction to the *Republic* is:

[16] Annas, J. *An Introduction to Plato's Republic* (Oxford: OUP, 1980).

See also:

[17] Cross, R. C. & Woozley, A. D. *Plato's Republic* (London: Macmillan, 1966).

Further useful reading on the topics discussed in this chapter may be found in:

[18] Crombie, I. M. *An Examination of Plato's Doctrines. Vol. II: Knowledge and Reality* (London: Routledge, 1963).

[19] Gosling, J. *Plato* (London: Routledge, 1973).

[20] Bambrough, R. (ed.) *New Essays on Plato and Aristotle* (London: Routledge, 1965).

[21] Allen, R. E. (ed.) *Studies in Plato's Metaphysics* (London: Routledge, 1965).

ARISTOTLE

The standard English version of Aristotle's works is:

[22] Smith, J. A. & Ross, W. D. (eds.) *The Works of Aristotle* (Oxford: OUP, 1910 rev. 1952).

Accurate English versions which keep close to the Greek may be found in:

[23] Ackrill, J. (ed.) *The Clarendon Aristotle* (Oxford: OUP, 1961–73).

Included in this series are:

[23a] Hamlyn, D. W. (tr.) Aristotle's *De Anima* (Oxford: OUP, 1968)

and

[23b] Barnes, J. (tr.) *Aristotle's Posterior Analytics* (Oxford: OUP, 1975).

The *Nicomachean Ethics* are translated in:

[24] Thompson, J. A. K. *The Ethics of Aristotle* rev. edn. by Barnes, J. (Harmondsworth: Penguin, 1976).

An excellent general introduction to Aristotle is:

[25] Ackrill, J. *Aristotle the Philosopher* (Oxford: OUP, 1981).

See also:

[26] Allan, D. J. *The Philosophy of Aristotle* (Oxford: OUP, 1952)

or the older but still useful:

[27] Ross, D. *Aristotle* (London: Methuen, rev. 1949).

A valuable collection of articles on Aristotle's philosophy of science is:

[28] Barnes, J., Schofield, M. & Sorabji, R. (eds.) *Articles on Aristotle: Vol. I: Science* (London: Duckworth, 1975). Other volumes deal with Ethics and Politics (II), Metaphysics (III) and Psychology and Aesthetics (IV).

For Aristotle's theory of scientific knowledge see:

[29] Berti, E. (ed.) *Aristotle on Science: The Posterior Analytics* (Padova: Antenore, 1981).

And for an excellent recent collection on Aristotle's ethical theory see:

[30] Rorty, A. O. (ed.) *Essays on Aristotle's Ethics* (Los Angeles: University of California Press, 1980).

CHAPTER 3

DESCARTES

The standard edition of the works of Descartes is:

[31] Adam, C. & Tannery, P. (eds.) *Oeuvres de Descartes* (Paris: Cerf, 1897–1913; repr. Paris: Vrin, 1957–76) twelve vols. (Known as 'AT'). References are to volume and page number (e.g. 'VI, 25').

A useful and scholarly three-volume edition is:

[32] Alquie, F. (ed.) *Descartes, Oeuvres Philosophiques* (Paris: Garnier, 1967).

The standard English translation (not entirely satisfactory and soon to be replaced) is the two-volume:

[33] Haldane, E. S. & Ross, G. T. R. *The Philosophical Works of Descartes* (Cambridge: CUP, 1911) (Known as 'HR'). References are to volume and page number (e.g. 'II, 205').

Not included in HR are:

[34] *Descartes' Philosophical Letters* tr. Kenny, A. (Oxford: OUP, 1970),

and

[35] *Descartes' Conversation with Burman* tr. Cottingham, J. (Oxford: OUP, 1976).

An excellent general introduction to Descartes' philosophy is:

[36] Kenny, A. *Descartes, A Study of his Philosophy* (New York: Random House, 1968).

Many stimulating insights may be found in:

[37] Williams, B. *Descartes, The Project of Pure Inquiry* (Harmondsworth: Penguin, 1978).

The best account of Descartes' metaphysics as set forth in the *Meditations* is:

[38] Wilson, M. *Descartes* (London: Routledge, 1980).

For a careful and judicious account of Descartes' conception of scientific inquiry, see:

[39] Clarke, D. M. *Descartes' Philosophy of Science* (Manchester: Manchester University Press, 1982).

Collections of critical essays on Descartes include:

[40] Doney, W. (ed.) *Descartes* (London: Macmillan, 1968).

[41] Butler, R.J. (ed.) *Cartesian Studies* (Oxford: Blackwell, 1972) and

[42] Hooker, M. (ed.) *Descartes, Critical and Interpretative Essays* (Baltimore: Johns Hopkins, 1978).

SPINOZA

The standard edition is:

[43] Gebhardt, C. (ed.) *Spinoza, Opera* (Heidelberg: Carl Winters Universitätsbuchhandlung, 1925) four vols.

The handiest English edition of Spinoza is:

[44] Elwes, R. H. M. *The Chief Works of Benedict de Spinoza* (New York: Dover, 1955) two vols.

An alternative is:

[45] Boyle, A. *Spinoza's Ethics and De Intellectus Emendatione* (London: Dent, 1910) (Everyman).

A very clear and informative general introduction to Spinoza is:

[46] Parkinson, G. H. R. *Spinoza* (Milton Keynes: Open University Press, 1983).

See also:

[47] Hampshire, S. *Spinoza* (Harmondsworth: Penguin, 1951).

A useful collection of critical essays is:

[48] Kashap, S. P. (ed.) *Studies in Spinoza* (Berkeley: University of California Press, 1972).

Further reading:

[49] Parkinson, G. H. R. *Spinoza's Theory of Knowledge* (Oxford: OUP, 1954).

[50] Wolfson, H. A. *The Philosophy of Spinoza* (1934; repr. New York: Schoken, 1969).

For consciousness and its relation to physiology see:

[51] Nagel, T. *Mortal Questions* (Cambridge: CUP, 1980), Ch.13 ('What is it like to be a bat?').

For a general introduction to seventeenth-century philosophical ideas see:

[52] Von Leyden, W. *Seventeenth-Century Metaphysics* (London: Duckworth, 1968).

LEIBNIZ

The standard edition is:

[53] Gerhardt, C. I. (ed.) *Die Philosophische Schriften von G. W. Leibniz* (Berlin: Weidman, 1875–90).

The full edition, still awaiting completion, is:

[54] *Leibniz: Sämtliche Schriften und Briefe* edited by the Deutsche Akadmie der Wissenschaften (Darmstadt & Berlin, 1923–).

The handiest English collection is:

[55] Parkinson, G. H. R. (ed.) *Leibniz: Philosophical Writings* (London: Dent, rev. 1973).

See also:

[56] Lucas, P. & Grint, L. *Leibniz, Discourse on Metaphysics* (Manchester: MUP, 1952).

Bibliography

[57] Schrecker P. & A. M. *Leibniz Monadology and Other Philosophical Essays* (New York: Bobbs Merrill, 1965).

[58] Huggard, E. M. *Leibniz' Theodicy* (London: Routledge, 1952).

[59] Matson, H. T. (tr.) *The Leibniz-Arnauld Correspondence* (Manchester: MUP, 1967).

A brief introduction covering many aspects of Leibniz' philosophy is:

[60] Rescher, N. *The Philosophy of Leibniz* (Englewood Cliffs: Prentice Hall, 1967).

See also:

[61] Van-Pearsen C. A. *Leibniz* (London: Faber, 1969)

and

[62] Broad, C. D. *Leibniz, An Introduction* (Cambridge: CUP, rev. 1975).

A more advanced discussion of Leibnizian metaphysics is:

[63] Parkinson, G. H. R. *Logic and Reality in Leibniz' Metaphysics* (Oxford: OUP, 1965).

Bertrand Russell's views on Leibniz appeared in:

[64] Russell, B. *A Critical Exposition of the Philosophy of Leibniz* (Cambridge: CUP, 1900; 2nd edn. London: Allen & Unwin, 1937).

A valuable collection of critical essays is:

[65] Frankfurt H. G. (ed.) *Leibniz* (New York: Doubleday, 1972).

For Leibniz' views on free will and determinism see:

[66] Parkinson, G. H. R. *Leibniz on Human Freedom* (Wiesbaden: Steiner, 1970).

CHAPTER 4

LOCKE

[67] Locke, John *Essay Concerning Human Understanding* (1690). ed. Nidditch, P.M. (Oxford: Clarendon, 1975).

Several abridged editions are available, some in paperback (e.g. the Fontana edition edited by Woozley, A. D.,

London: Collins, 1964). Numbering by Book, Chapter and sections is common to all editions.

For critical assessments of Locke see:

[68] Mabbott, J. D. *John Locke* (London: Macmillan, 1973).

[69] Yolton, J. W. *John Locke and the Way of Ideas* (Oxford: Clarendon, 1968).

[70] Bennett, J. *Locke, Berkeley, Hume* (Oxford: OUP, 1971).

Leibniz' critique of Locke was first published posthumously in 1785 as:

[71] Leibniz, G. W. *Nouveaux Essais sur l'entendement humain* translated in [55] above.

HUME

[72] Hume, David *A Treatise of Human Nature* (1739–40). The standard edition is by Selby-Bigge, L. A. (Oxford: OUP, revised third edn. Oxford: OUP, 1975). References by book, part and section are common to all editions.

[73] Hume, David *Enquiry concerning Human Understanding* (the 'First Enquiry') 1748 ed. Selby-Bigge, L. A. (3rd edn. Oxford: OUP, 1975). References to section numbers, and parts of sections, are common to all editions.

For critical assessments of Hume see:

[74] Macnabb, D. *David Hume* (Oxford: Blackwell, 2nd edn. 1966),

[75] Flew, A. *Hume's Philosophy of Belief* (London: Routledge, 1961),

[76] Kemp Smith, N. *The Philosophy of David Hume* (London, 1941). See also Bennett [70].

A useful collection of introductory essays is:

[77] Pears, D. F. (ed.) *David Hume, A Symposium* (London: Macmillan, 1966).

A more advanced collection is:

[78] Chappell, V. C. (ed.) *Hume* (London: Macmillan, 1968).

For a defence of the Humean view of causation see:

[79] Mackie, J. *The Cement of the Universe* (Oxford: OUP, 1980)

and, for a strongly critical view:

[80] Harré, R. & Madden, E. H. *Causal Powers* (Oxford: Blackwell, 1975).

KANT

The standard edition of Kant's writings is:

[81] *Kant's gesammelte Schriften* (Berlin: Reimer de Gruyter, 1902–).

The standard English version of the *Kritik der Reinen Vernunft* (1781; 2nd edn. 1787) is:

[82] Kemp Smith, N., *Immanuel Kant's Critique of Pure Reason* (London: Macmillan, 1929). The system of marginal references to the first edition (A) and the second edition (B) is used in all editions and translations of the *Critique*.

Kant's *Prolegomena* (1783) is translated in:

[83] Lucas P. G. *Kant's Prolegomena to Every Future Metaphysics* (Manchester: MUP, 1953).

For a sound summary of Kant's arguments see:

[84] Scruton, R. *Kant* (Oxford: OUP, 1982).

More detailed analysis and criticism may be found in:

[85] Walker, R. C. S. *Kant* (London: Routledge, 1978) and

[86] Bennett, J. F. *Kant's Analytic* (Cambridge: CUP, 1966).

CHAPTER 5

HEGEL

The standard editions are:

[87] *Sämtliche Werke* (eds.) Lasson, G. & Hoffmeister, J. (Leipzig: Meiner, 1928–) and

[88] *Sämtliche Werke* (ed.) Glockner, H. (Stuttgart: Jubiläumausgabe 1972–).

Hegel's *Phänomenologie des Geistes* is translated in:

[89] Miller, A. V. *Hegel's Phenomenology of Spirit* (Oxford: OUP, 1977).

Various parts of the *Encyclopädie* appear in English as:

[90] Wallace, W. (tr.) *The Logic of Hegel* (Oxford: OUP, 1892),

[91] Miller, A. V. (tr.) *Hegel's Philosophy of Nature* (Oxford: OUP, 1970),

[92] Wallace, W. (tr.) *Hegel's Philosophy of Mind* (Oxford: OUP, 1894).

The *Naturrecht und Staatswissenschaft im Grundrisse*, and *Grundlinien der Philosophie des Rechts* appear as:

[93] Knox, T. M. *Hegel's Philosophy of Right* (Oxford: OUP, 1952).

A valuable account of Hegel's thought is:

[94] Taylor, C. *Hegel* (Cambridge: CUP, 1975).

See also:

[95] Norman, R. *Hegel's Phenomenology* (London: Sussex University Press, 1976).

An excellent collection of critical writings is:

[96] MacIntyre, A. (ed.) *Hegel: A Collection of Critical Essays* (New York: Doubleday, 1972).

A useful reference work for nineteenth-century philosophy is:

[97] Wintle, J. (ed.) *Makers of Nineteenth Century Culture* (London: Routledge, 1982).

and, for the twentieth century,

[98] Wintle, J. (ed.) *Makers of Modern Culture* (London: Routledge, 1981).

RUSSELL AND WITTGENSTEIN

[99] Russell, B. *The Problems of Philosophy* (1912; repr. Oxford: OUP, 1967).

Also of interest are:

[100] Russell, B. *Mysticism and Logic* (London: Longmans, 1917)

and

[101] Russell, B. *My Philosophical Development* (London: Allen & Unwin, 1959).

Helpful exegesis of Russell's views may be found in:

[102] Pears, D. F. *Bertrand Russell and the British Tradition in Philosophy* (London: Fontana, 1967)

and in

[103] Sainsbury, R. M. *Russell* (London: Routledge, 1979).

Wittgenstein's 'Tractatus' (*Logisch-Philosophische Abhandlung*), 1921 is published as:

[104] Wittgenstein, L. *Tractatus Logico-Philosophicus* tr. Pears, D. F. & McGuinness, B. F. (London: Routledge, 1961). Each proposition in the *Tractatus* is numbered by Wittgenstein by means of a decimal system.

See also:

[105] Copi, F. M. & Beard, R. N. *Essays on Wittgenstein's Tractatus* (London: Routledge, 1961)

and, for an elegant general introduction to Wittgenstein:

[106] Kenny, A. *Wittgenstein* (Harmondsworth: Penguin, 1975).

LOGICAL POSITIVISM

[107] Ayer, A. J. *Language, Truth and Logic* (London: Gollancz, 1936; 2nd edn. 1946).

An excellent collection of sources is:

[108] Ayer, A. J. (ed.) *Logical Positivism* (New York: Free Press, 1959).

Further material may be found in:

[109] Hanfling, O. (ed.) *Essential Readings in Logical Positivism* (Oxford: Blackwell, 1981).

QUINE AND KRIPKE

Quine's 'Two dogmas of empiricism' (1951) appears in:

[110] Quine, W. V. O. *From a Logical Point of View* (Cambridge, Mass.: Harvard UP, 1951; rev. edn. New York: Harper & Row, 1963).

Quine's later work (in which there are a certain number of modifications to the views expressed in 'Two dogmas') includes:

[111] Quine, W. V. O. *Word and Object* (Cambridge: MIT Press, 1960)

and

[112] Quine, W. V. O. *The Ways of Paradox* (Cambridge, Mass.: Harvard UP, 2nd edn. 1976).

For criticism of Quine see:

[113] Davidson, D. & Hintika, J. (eds.) *Words and Objections: Essays on the Work of W. V. O. Quine* (Dordrecht: Reidel, 1969).

Kripke's celebrated lectures were published as:

[114] Kripke, S. *Naming and Necessity* (1972; rev. edn. Oxford: Blackwell, 1980).

For discussion of Kripke's theory of meaning see:

[115] Platts, M. *Ways of Meaning* (London: Routledge, 1979)

and the collection of critical essays in:

[116] Schwartz, S. P. (ed.) *Naming, Necessity and Natural Kinds* (Ithaca: Cornell University Press, 1976).

See also:

[117] Putnam, H. *Mind, Language and Reality* (Cambridge: CUP, 1975).

CHOMSKY

The most accessible text is:

[118] Chomsky, N. *Language and Mind* (New York: Harcourt, Brace & World, 1968).

See also:

[119] Chomsky, N. 'Knowledge of Language' *Times Lit. Sup.* 15 May 1969.

For Chomsky's innatism see:

[120] Chomsky, N. 'Recent Contributions to the Theory of Innate Ideas', repr. in Stitch, S. P. (ed.) *Innate Ideas* (Berkeley: University of California Press, 1975).

For the empiricist view against which Chomsky reacted see:

[121] Skinner, B. F. *Verbal Behaviour* (New York: Appleton, 1957).

A useful collection of critical essays on Chomsky's work is:

[122] Hook, S. (ed.) *Language and Philosophy* (New York: NYUP, 1969). See especially Nagel, T. 'Linguistics and Epistemology' which develops the parallel between linguistic and digestive powers.

See also:

[123] Hacking, I. *Why Does Language Matter to Philosophy?* (Cambridge: CUP, 1975), p.57ff.

And, for a brief general introduction to Chomsky:

[124] Lyons, J. *Chomsky* (London: Collins/Fontana, 1970).

RATIONALISM AND ETHICS

For the eighteenth-century background see the following works:

[125] Clarke, Samuel *A Discourse concerning the Unchangeable Obligations of Natural Religion* (1706) repr. in

[126] Raphael, D. D. (ed.) *British Moralists* (Oxford: Clarendon, 1969).

[127] Hume, David *Enquiry Concerning the Principles of Morals* (1751) edited in Selby-Bigge, L. A., *David Hume, Enquiries* (3rd edn. Oxford: OUP, 1974).

[128] Kant, Immanuel *Grundlegung zur Metaphysik der Sitten*, trans. in Paton, H. J. *The Moral Law* (London: Hutchinson, 1948).

For further discussion of Kant's examples see Walker [85] above.

For the emotive theory see:

[129] Stevenson, C. *Ethics and Language* (New Haven: Yale Univ. Press, 1944)

and

[130] Urmson, J. *The Emotive Theory of Ethics* (London: Hutchinson, 1968).

R.M. Hare's views on universalizability are contained in:

[131] Hare, R. M. *Freedom and Reason* (Oxford: OUP, 1962)

and

[132] Hare, R. M. *Moral Thinking* (Oxford: OUP, 1981).

The subjectivist case is elegantly stated in:

[133] Mackie, J. L. *Ethics* (Harmondsworth: Penguin, 1977).

For a contrasting view see:

[134] Bambrough, R. *Moral Scepticism and Moral Knowledge* (London: Routledge, 1979).

The term 'naturalistic fallacy' was first used in:

[135] Moore, G. E. *Principia Ethica* (Cambridge: CUP, 1903).

For Searle's paper 'How to derive "ought" from "is"' (1964), and some searching criticisms of it, see:

[136] Hudson, W. (ed.) *The Is/Ought Question* (London: Macmillan, 1979).

A 'neo-naturalist' position is developed in:

[137] Midgley, M. *Beast and Man* (Sussex: Harvester, 1978) and criticized in:

[138] Cottingham, J. 'Neonaturalism and its pitfalls', in *Philosophy* (1983).

Sartre's views are expounded in:

[139] Sartre, J–P. *L'Etre et le Néant* (1943) tr. Barnes, H. (London: Methuen, 1957).

For more on Sartre's philosophy see:

[140] Murdoch, I. *Sartre* (London: Bowes, 1953),

[141] Warnock, M. *The Philosophy of Sartre* (London: Hutchinson, 1965) and

[142] Manser A. *Sartre* (London: Athlone, 1966).

RATIONALISM AND SCIENTIFIC METHOD

[143] Popper, K. *Logik der Forschung* (1934) English edn. *The Logic of Scientific Discovery* (London: Hutchinson, 1959; repr. 1968).

See also Popper's own excellent introduction to his views:

[144] Popper, K. *Autobiography of Karl Popper* (Illinois: Open Court, 1974); rev. edn. entitled *The Unended Quest* (London: Fontana, 1976).

Bibliography

The two most important sources for the recent 'revolution' in the philosophy of science are:

[145] Kuhn, T. *The Structure of Scientific Revolutions* (Chicago: Chicago University Press, 1962; 2nd edn. 1970)

and

[146] Feyerabend, P. 'Explanation, Reduction and Empiricism' in Feigl, H. & Maxwell, G. (eds) *Minnesota Studies in the Philosophy of Science* (Minneapolis: University of Minnesota Press, 1962).

Further sources, together with a useful introduction, appear in:

[147] Hacking, I. (ed.) *Scientific Revolutions* (Oxford: OUP, 1981).

Kuhn's later writings include:

[148] Kuhn, T. *The Essential Tension: Selected Studies in Scientific Tradition and Change* (Chicago: Chicago UP, 1977).

Further valuable material appears in:

[149] Lakatos, I. & Musgrave, A. *Criticism and the Growth of Knowledge* (Cambridge: CUP, 1970).

See also:

[150] Papineau, D. 'Thinking up reality', *Times Lit. Sup.*, 29 October 1982.

For the 'hermeneutic' approach to philosophy see:

[151] Rorty, R. *Philosophy and the Mirror of Nature* (Oxford: Blackwell, 1980).

The self-refuting argument is quoted from:

[152] Berg, C. *Deep Analysis* (London: Allen & Unwin, 1946)

and discussed in:

[153] Flew, A. 'A Strong Programme for the Sociology of Belief', *Inquiry*, Vol. 25.

For more on self-refutation and other issues discussed in this section, see:

[154] Hesse, M. *Revolutions and Reconstructions in the Philosophy of Science* (Brighton: Harvester, 1980).

The 'social basis' of logic is discussed in:

[155] Winch, P. *The Idea of a Social Science* (London: Routledge, 1958).

For further discussion of the claims of relativism see:

[156] Hollis, M. & Lukes, S. *Rationality and Relativism* (Oxford: Blackwell, 1982)
and
[157] Newton-Smith, W. H. *The Rationality of Science* (London: Routledge, 1981).

Index

Philosophy/Religion in Paladin Books

The Sound of the One Hand £1.50 ☐
Yoel Hoffman
Never before has it been possible for an English-speaking reader to experience the profound exchange which occurs between a Zen master and his student. Here, for the first time, is the series of questions or 'Koans', together with their answers, through which the Zen master initiates the novice into the wisdom of Zen.

The Aquarian Conspiracy £2.95 ☐
Marilyn Ferguson
Slowly, almost unnoticed, a revolution is taking place. A leaderless but powerful network is working to bring about radical change in our culture. Its members have broken with certain key elements of Western thought, and they may even have broken continuity with history and are working to create a different kind of society based on a vastly enlarged concept of human potential.

A Smile in the Mind's Eye £1.95 ☐
Lawrence Durrell
Lawrence Durrell has had a lifelong interest in and sympathy for the philosophy of Taoism. In this entertaining, charming and informative short memoir he gives us a totally absorbing account of an inner journey to growth and spiritual enlightenment.

To order direct from the publisher just tick the titles you want and fill in the order form. **PAL13182**

Psychology/Life Sciences in Paladin Books

The Life Science   £1.25 □
P B and J S Medawar
As the frontiers of biological knowledge continue to be extended,
this is a timely critical appraisal of the central thinking of biologists.

The Cosmic Clocks   £1.50 □
Michel Gauquelin
The classic book which first established the links between the
ancient art of astrology and the modern science of the rhythms of the
universe and of all life, the time patterns that are etched into the
personality of every living being.

The Natural History of the Mind   £2.50 □
Gordon Rattray Taylor
A lucid and readable round-up of the widely scattered research that
has been carried out on the human mind.

Body Time   £1.25 □
Gay Gaer Luce
A study of the biological rhythms that influence our feelings and
performances.

The Selfish Gene   £1.95 ☑
Richard Dawkins
A provocative appraisal of social biology — the genetics of
selfishness and altruism. 'This important book could hardly be more
exciting.' *The Economist*

To order direct from the publisher just tick the titles you want
and fill in the order form.